W9-BSQ-811

FLYING HIGHER

FLYING HIGHER

The Women Airforce Service Pilots of World War II

BY WANDA LANGLEY

LINNET BOOKS
NORTH HAVEN, CONNECTICUT

First published 2002 as a Linnet Book,
an imprint of The Shoe String Press, Inc.,
2 Linsley Street, North Haven, Connecticut 06473.
www.shoestringpress.com

Library of Congress Cataloging-in-Publication Data

Langley, Wanda.
    Flying higher : the Women Airforce Service Pilots of World War II /
by Wanda Langley.
        p. cm.
    Includes bibliographical references and index.
    ISBN 0–208–02506–5 (alk. paper)
    1. Women Airforce Service Pilots (U.S.) 2. Women air pilots—
United States—History—20th century. 3. World War, 1939–1945—
Aerial operations, American. 4. World War, 1939–1945—Women—
United States. I. Title.

D810.W7 W345 2002
940.54'4973—dc21

                                                2002016109

The paper in this publication meets the minimum requirements
of American National Standard for Information Sciences–
Permanence of Paper for Printed Library Materials,
ANSI-Z39.1984 ∞

Designed by Dutton & Sherman
Printed in the United States of America

To the Women Airforce Pilots of World War II,
who knew the value of service
and
To Dan, who knows the value of history

CONTENTS

Acknowledgments ix

ONE

On Solid Ground 1

TWO

Ready to Fly 8

THREE

The Blond Bombshell 15

FOUR

Fighting for the Right to Fly 24

FIVE

Up in the Air 29

SIX

Bucket of Bolts and the Hood 38

SEVEN

Crossing the Country 46

EIGHT

Silver Wings and Santiago Blue 53

NINE

Careful Where You Aim, Sir 63

TEN

You Call This Plane Fixed? 71

ELEVEN

We Can Fly Anything in This Man's Army 79

TWELVE

Other Planes, Other Places 89

THIRTEEN

Flying Higher 99

Epilogue 107

Appendixes 115

Notes 121

Glossary 123

Bibliography 125

Index 129

ACKNOWLEDGMENTS

Numerous people helped with this project. A few deserve special mention:

William Leary, Professor of Military History and former Charles E. Lindbergh Scholar at the Smithsonian's National Air and Space Museum, who gave technical expertise and professional encouragement;

Nancy Marshall Durr, Dawn Letson, and Tracey Mac Gowan of Texas Woman's University, who provided assistance during my research in the WASP archives at Blagg-Huey Library, The Woman's Collection; Elizabeth MacKethan Magid and Ken Magid for permission to use the poem, "Celestial Flight"; Anne Noggle for permission to use an excerpt from her poem, "Sky High";

44-W-2 WASPs Kate Adams, Doris Hamaker, Lorraine Rodgers, and Fran Tuchband, who read and approved portions of the text; Verda-Mae Jennings, Lois Cutler, Leona Zimmer, Minkie Heckman, Sadie Goot, Mimi Segall, Ruth Petry, Toby Felker, Sid Bergemann, Ruth Adams, Anne Lesnikowski, Annabelle Moss,

Joanne Orr, Madeline O'Donnell, and Ruth Kunkle, who shared their training and service experiences;

Other WASPs Eleanor Wortz, Margaret Riviere, Marion Hodgson, Captola Johnson, Peg Roberts, Virginia Waterer, June Drew, Doris Tanner, Carol Selfridge, Martha Boshart, Rita Stump, and Florine Watson, who also provided helpful information;

Gail Karwoski, Bettye Stroud, Lori Hammer, and Dan Langley, whose critique and support made this book possible;

The late Jean Hascall Cole, who introduced me to the class of 44-W-2 with her book, *Women Pilots of World War II,* which lent a great deal to my research for this book. Her tapes and transcripts reside in a collection in her name at Texas Woman's University, The Woman's Collection;

Roy Michell, Jr., whose memories brought Marie Michell Robinson to life once more.

"*Courage is the price that life exacts for granting peace. The soul that knows it not, knows no release from little things. . . .*"

—AMELIA EARHART

"*Adventure is a state of mind—and spirit, it comes with faith, for with complete faith there is no fear of what faces you in life or death.*"

—JACQUELINE COCHRAN

ONE

On Solid Ground

If you have a daughter, teach her how to fly.

—WASP SONG

The cattle truck stopped in front of the Bluebonnet Hotel and Marie Michell stepped on board. Other young women followed her. They watched their feet as they climbed the steps and laughed at how impractical high heels were on such an unlikely carriage. When the women and their baggage were safely stowed, the driver steered his truck toward Avenger Field.

On that September 6 morning in 1943, the citizens of Sweetwater, Texas saw long, military buses, dubbed "cattle trucks," rattling west to the all-female pilot training base at Avenger Field. They were carrying young women who hoped to become Women Airforce Service Pilots (WASP). This group was the tenth class of eighteen that entered the pilot training program. They would be known as 44-W-2, the second class of women to graduate in 1944.

As they bumped along, Marie Michell resumed her conversation with Kit MacKethan from North Carolina. They had met the

1

Marie Michell stands ready to board her training plane. Zoot suits (coveralls) and parachutes were standard items for pilots. Closed-toe shoes were required but styles were not regulated for WASP trainees. The piece of tape on Marie's right leg was a reminder to log her flying hours in her logbook. *Courtesy of Roy Michell, Jr.*

day before on a train coming into Sweetwater. Kit had noticed pretty Marie with her delicate features, auburn hair, and blue eyes. They were delighted to find both were going to the women's pilot training program. And other women on the train were just as eager to get to Avenger Field.

These women pilots had grown up hearing about Charles Lindbergh, who was the first pilot to fly solo across the Atlantic Ocean and a national hero. They had read about the famous female fliers, Amelia Earhart and Jacqueline "Jackie" Cochran, and other early women aviators who had set long-distance and racing records.

Before America entered World War II in 1941, most women stayed at home, tending households and caring for children, while their husbands had outside jobs earning money to support their families. Although few women flew planes, the women in 44-W-2 had scraped and saved to take flight lessons and had earned their private pilots' licenses. Other than a love of flying, these women had little in common. They were brought together at this time and in this place by a great war.

By 1943, World War II encompassed most of the globe. In Europe and Africa, heavy Allied bombers dropped their deadly loads on Hitler's German and Mussolini's Italian forces. Sleek American fighter planes skirmished with agile Japanese *Zeros* across the Pacific Ocean. At home and abroad, giant cargo planes had their bellies filled with men and materiel for the war effort. Increasingly the war was being waged in the air. Male military pilots were desperately needed for combat duty, and this left a serious shortage of pilots to fly new planes from factories to American air bases and port cities for shipment overseas.

The Army Air Forces called upon women pilots to close this gap; Marie Michell and her companions answered that call. When they heard Jacqueline Cochran was recruiting licensed women fliers for the Women Airforce Service Pilots (WASP), they applied. These women had to meet certain standards set by Director Cochran: a minimum height of 5 feet, 2 $\frac{1}{2}$ inches; an age minimum of 18 $\frac{1}{2}$; they could have no less than 35 hours flying time; and had to pass a battery of mental and physical tests. Jackie Cochran and her staff interviewed every applicant to determine her "good moral character."

Those who were accepted received a letter from Cochran telling them when to report to Avenger Field. Their pay would be $150 a month (about $1,560 in today's money), minus $1.65 ($17.16) a day for room and board. The women pilots were classified as Civil Service employees in the United States government. Because she was a civilian, each woman had to pay her own way to Avenger Field and buy her own uniform.

As the cattle truck topped a mesa, the women saw a treeless plain dotted with clumps of brown grass, gray-green prickly pear cacti, and dark green tumbleweeds. And sand—everywhere, sand. This goes-on-forever land was nothing like where Marie Michell had grown up.

Marie was born in Detroit, Michigan, in 1924. She had lived in many places during her young life: Birmingham, Michigan; Larchmont, New York; and the larger cities of New Orleans and Chicago, among others. Her parents had divorced when Marie was about six and her mother had remarried. Marie and her older brother, Roy, lived with their mother and stepfather and moved when his work took him to these different places. But Marie stayed in touch with her father and remained close to him.

After a year or two of attending high school in Chicago, Marie was sent to a finishing school in Maryland where she graduated. Unknown to her family, she took flying lessons while there and came back to Chicago with her private pilot's license.

After a brief stint as a dancer at a Chicago dinner club, and then a few semesters at Vanderbilt University in Tennessee, Marie went back to Chicago to accumulate more flying hours. She also

Fifinella, the WASP emblem, stands watch at the entrance to Avenger Field, ready to chase away any gremlins that might bring bad luck. *Courtesy of The Woman's Collection, Texas Woman's University*

trained to become a Link instructor, training pilots to fly by instruments. When she heard about the WASP program, she realized what she really wanted to do. Now, she was at Sweetwater to learn how to fly military aircraft, and she was thrilled to be there.

The truck slowed at a gate for checkpoint. On top of the gate flew Fifinella, the insignia of the WASP. Walt Disney, who had created Fifinella as a cartoon character, lent the fanciful sprite to the WASP to use as their emblem. The creature had blue wings and wore an orange jacket, orange boots, black elbow-length gloves, and tight yellow pants. On her horned head was a yellow helmet with blue goggles.

The guard waved the truck through the gate. When it finally stopped at the white administration building, the women cheered and shouted. A dusty wind hit them when they stepped down, and they grabbed at their skirts with one hand and their hair or hats with the other. They could hear the American flag whipping and snapping from the flagpole.

But their eyes were drawn overhead. The sky was layered with planes, and the drone of their engines sounded like music. Planes were taking off and landing, turning in slow loops and fast spins, and flying upside down and right side up. This was why Marie and the other women pilots had come. They wanted to serve their country, yes, but they also wanted to fly.

They were met by women student officers from the upper classes, who marched them to the training theater for processing. Once inside, they were greeted by the military staff of the United States Army Air Forces. The base adjutant, an officer in charge, ordered the women to line up and to look at the person on either side. Then he told them that every two out of three people would "wash out" before they had finished the twenty-seven-week training program. Dorothy "Sadie" Hawkins, a native Texan, looked at the person on her right and her left and thought, "Poor things."[1] It never occurred to her that she might be one of the ones to quit or be eliminated from the program. The Army Air Forces underestimated the determination of these women.

There were 112 women pilots in the class of 44-W-2. They ranged in age from 18 ½ to 28, and they came from all regions in the United States. Some were from privileged backgrounds; others not so privileged. A few were married. Most had some college education. Their flying experience ranged from thirty-five to several hundred hours.

All had done whatever was necessary to get into the WASP program. Many had worked at low-paying jobs and saved their lunch money to pay for flying lessons. A few (at least two who would admit it years later) had added extra time on their flight logbooks to get the required thirty-five hours.

Others slid by on the physical exam. Kit MacKethan wore a heavy metal belt under her clothes to add pounds to her slight frame. Jean Hascall from Vermont was a little short of the height requirement. The medical examiner noticed her standing on her toes. He asked, "What's the matter? Not tall enough? How tall do you want to be?"

When Jean told him that the requirement was 5 feet, 2 ½ inches, he said, "Well, honey, that's just what we'll make you."[2]

Nellie Henderson, who held a private pilot's license from Louisiana, was nearsighted. The examiners noticed she was squinting at the eye chart and they said, "You don't see very well, do you?"

"No," she said, "But don't tell anybody."[3]

So they passed her. But she did have flying glasses with corrections in them.

Suddenly a tiny, bird-like woman entered the room and hopped up on a table. "Welcome to Avenger Field," she said. "I'm Leni Leoti Clark Deaton, your chief staff executive or establishment officer here."[4]

TWO

Ready to Fly

We live in the wind and the sand . . . and our eyes are on the stars.

—MOTTO OF AVENGER FIELD

As chief establishment officer at Avenger Field, Leni Leoti "Deedie" Clark Deaton was responsible for looking after the trainees' welfare; she had six women establishment officers on her staff to assist her. Deedie Deaton reported directly to Jacqueline Cochran, Director of the Women Airforce Service Pilots. The two women respected and worked closely with each other.

Mrs. Deaton had a long career with the Red Cross and had served as dean of women at the Red Cross Aquatic School. She came to her present job when her pilot cousin recommended her to Jackie Cochran, who needed an administrator for the new women's pilot training program at Houston, Texas. Mrs. Deaton had no intention of leaving her job or her husband and teenage son. But she was persuaded by Miss Cochran, who, as Deedie put it, "could sell a hot brick in hell."[5]

The new training program, officially designated the 319th Army Air Forces Flying Training Detachment (319th AAFFTD), was due to start in November 1942. Mrs. Deaton was hired two weeks before the program started. When she arrived at Houston, she found that no housing, transportation, dining, or medical facilities existed for the female trainees—and twenty-eight members of class 43-W-1 (the first women to graduate in 1943) were already on their way! She finally found housing in "tourist courts" and in private homes.

Mrs. Deaton then directed her attention to solving the next big problem: transportation. To get the trainees from their living quarters to flight training, she found a bus used by a Tyrolean band. This blue bus, painted with edelweiss and sporting a red and white striped awning, transported them until the military trucks arrived.

Other obstacles abounded. The bus broke down frequently; at the Howard Hughes Municipal Airport where flight training was held, there were no meal facilities, and the only women's bathroom was in the airport terminal; there were not enough military planes; and worst of all, many flying days were lost when fog rolled into Houston. Meanwhile, new classes continued to arrive monthly.

Director Cochran learned of a military training base in Sweetwater, about 175 miles west of Fort Worth, that was being evacuated. Cochran and her military superiors decided to move the training program to Avenger Field because the base had adequate facilities, and the weather permitted 300 flying days in the year.

The first women of the 319th AAFFTD—"Woofteds," they called themselves—graduated April 24, 1943. They were sent to four different bases with the Army Air Forces Air Transport Command, Ferrying Division, for further training on the military planes they would ferry from the factories to air bases and port cities. They were supervised by Nancy Love, head of the Women's Auxiliary Ferry Squadron (WAFS), another civilian group of pilots within the military. The Woofteds, who averaged over 200 flying hours even before entering Cochran's program, proved to be superb pilots, and their base commanders sent back highly favorable reports. The new women's pilot-training program would fly.

Still, the women pilots encountered hostility as did other minorities such as African Americans, Native Americans, Hispanics, and Japanese Americans who served in the military during World War II. The anger directed toward them came from the fact that women and minorities stepped out—and up—from the lower-status roles that society had assigned them at the time. They had to prove over and over that they could, and would, do their jobs well. Their courage to face prejudice and discrimination sprang from confidence in their own abilities and the recognition that their country needed them.

On May 23, 1943, classes 43-W-2 and 43-W-3 in Houston climbed into their training planes and flew to Sweetwater. The Army Air Forces redesignated the training program at Sweetwater as the 318th AAFFTD for administrative purposes. Some male cadets still remained at the base when the female pilots arrived, and for a six-week period, both men and women occupied Avenger Field. Typical of the segregation of the sexes at that time, the men and women had separate barracks, trained at different hangers, occupied different classrooms, and ate at opposite ends of the mess hall. The military commanding officer at Avenger Field was not enthusiastic about the women's arrival. When Mrs. Deaton asked him what he wanted her to do, he told her to keep the women out of his hair.

Many in the military shared the commander's attitude toward the women pilots. Some did not believe that women were capable of handling the heavier, more powerful military planes. Others felt their own positions were threatened. And still others felt that women had no business being in a "man's army" and should instead be at home, tending children and running households. The women pilots would have to work harder and show they could fly planes "the Army way."

The next commander at Avenger Field was Major Urban who had a more tolerant and professional view of the women trainees under his charge. He was assisted by an adjutant and a staff of nine military officers, who made the final flight checks on the women as they completed each level of pilot training. These officers also taught subjects on military service customs—necessary because the women, though civilians, would serve on Army Air Forces bases.

Two flight surgeons—doctors with at least one year of medical practice and fifty hours flying time—were also part of the military staff. One of the physicians, Lt. Nels O. Monserud, was conducting an important medical research project. The air surgeon of the Army Air Forces and Director Cochran wanted a study of the effects that a woman's physiological and psychological makeup had on flight. One of the tests was to determine if a woman's menstrual cycle affected her flying performance, a commonly held belief in and out of the military. Each month, every woman had to fill out a form, reporting her menses to Lieutenant Monserud. He checked this information against the regular evaluations from the flight instructors. The women trainees hated this invasion of privacy. They were convinced the aim of the program was to determine if they were pregnant.

The military officer the trainees saw most often was 1st Lt. William LaRue, physical director, an energetic and humorous fellow. He conducted four hours of physical training during the week, plus one hour of close-order drill. He put the women through the same Army Air Forces physical regimen that the male cadets went through. Trainees endured the grueling workouts and emerged in superb physical condition.

Flight One wearing "Urban's Turbans." *Bottom row* (from left): Susie Clarke, unidentified, Mary Ellen Keil, Kay Cleverly, Fran Laraway, Marjorie Johnson, Sadie Hawkins. *Second row*: Jean Hascall, Kate Lee Harris, Ruth Adams, Nellie Henderson. *Third row*: Margaret Ehlers, Ann Craft, Betty LeFevre, Millie Grossman, Kay Herman, Leona Golbinec, Anne Berry. *Top row*: Gini Dulaney, Minkie Heckman, Marjorie Gilbert, Twila Edwards, and Muriel Lindstrom. *Courtesy of The Woman's Collection, Texas Woman's University*

A private company, Aviation Enterprises, Inc., had a government contract to provide the civilian flight and ground school instructors and to hire the many people needed to run an army base. Ground instructors taught principles of aviation and mechanics. Most were college graduates with teaching experience. They taught Morse code, navigation, simulated flight, aeronautics, math, physics, engine maintenance, and meteorology. The 400-hour curriculum was the equivalent of a college graduate program. The courses were the same as those given to the male cadet pilots, except the program was completed in less time.

For instruction, each class was divided into two fairly equal groups, alphabetically by last name. Flight One consisted of trainees A-L; Flight Two, from M-Z. Each group had a class squadron commander and a flight lieutenant, chosen by the trainees. One week, Flight One would fly in the morning while Flight Two attended ground school; the following week, they switched. A trainee could wash out of flight or ground school at any time.

The class of 44-W-2 was immediately plunged into this daily schedule:

6:00 A.M.	Reveille, wake up
6:30	Formation and roll call
7:00	Breakfast
8:00	Back to quarters
9:00	Flight/ground school/physical training
12–2:00 P.M.	Lunch
1:00	Flight/ground school/physical training
6:00	Dinner
7:00	Study, write letters
9:30	All trainees in their rooms
10:00 P.M.	Lights out, taps
Saturday	Inspection in the morning, free time
	1:00 A.M. curfew
Sunday	Free time
	Lights out at 10 P.M.

Trainees were assigned six to a room, which was called a "bay." A bathroom or latrine was between two bays; twelve women shared two toilets and two showers. They slept on army cots with thin mattresses. Each trainee had a small, open closet and a foot-locker to store her belongings.

For work uniforms, they were issued men's coveralls. Nicknamed "zoot suits," they were made of heavy cotton twill in sizes forty-four and up. As the wearers walked, their seats swished behind them. They belted the coveralls and rolled up the legs. Dress uniforms, which the women were required to buy, consisted of khaki slacks, matching caps, and white blouses.

Hair had to be contained because of the possibility of long tresses getting caught in machinery. When 44-W-2 arrived, trainees wore hairnets. A short time later, the decree came down that trainees had to wear white turbans. They were promptly dubbed "Urban's Turbans." The women hated them.

Then there were the personal conduct rules set down by WASP Director Jacqueline Cochran. Demerits were given for minor infractions—not having hair contained, failure to have lights out after 10, being out of formation, and others. A certain number of demerits led to loss of weekend privileges; seventy-five demerits resulted in washout. Mrs. Deaton enforced the rules and made no exceptions.

Two rules were most important and carried the gravest consequence: no alcohol on base and no dating the instructors. Any trainee caught would be sent home immediately. Miss Cochran could not chance any breath of scandal. She knew her Army Air Forces superiors—and many civilians—were watching this great experiment, the first in United States aviation. Some observers expected this program to fail. Any controversy could bring it to a halt. But trainees did not know this at the time; they called Avenger Field "Cochran's Convent."

When 44-W-2 arrived, Mrs. Deaton already had her hands full preparing for the September 11 graduation of 43-W-5. Jackie Cochran almost always flew in to attend the ceremonies, often piloting her own plane. On graduation morning, the phone rang with the news that Miss Cochran's plane had taken off from Fort Worth. Word quickly spread around the office that Jacqueline Cochran, Director of Women Airforce Service Pilots, was coming.

THREE

The Blond Bombshell

I never thought of myself as ordinary.

—JACQUELINE COCHRAN

As Marie Michell and the other Avenger trainees marched past the reviewing platform that September graduation morning, they saw Jackie Cochran standing at attention. She was stylishly dressed, with a small hat perched on top of her blond hair. In her mid-thirties, she was prettier than her pictures. Marie and her classmates knew of Jackie's flying achievements. What the trainees did not know was how much the famed aviator's drive and determination fueled her many accomplishments.

Jackie Cochran went through life at full throttle. She was born in northern Florida of uncertain date (1905-1910) and parentage; even her birth name is unknown. She lived with a foster family in the squalid conditions of the sawmill camps—on Sawdust Road, as she called it.

Her family lived in an unpainted house with paper covering the cracks in the walls. To see at night, they lit "mojo lamps"— hollow cornstalks stuffed with cloth wicks that rested in oil-bottomed jars. Food consisted mostly of mullet fish and sowbelly. Jackie wore clothes made from flour sacks and pumped water to wash herself. About the influence of her early hardscrabble life, she later said, "Whatever I am is elemental and the beginnings of it all have their roots in Sawdust Road. I might have been born in a hovel but I determined to travel with the wind and the stars."[6] Jackie learned early to fend and fight.

Jackie's formal education was limited, a fact she deplored all her life. Three days after entering school in the first grade, the teacher whipped her and she struck back. She chose to stay home the rest of the year, doing as she pleased. The next year, Jackie had a pretty new teacher who taught her to read. She also bought the ragamuffin child her first new dress. Jackie adored her. After two years, the teacher did not return, and neither did Jackie. But she never stopped learning.

When she was 8, her family moved to Columbus, Georgia to seek work in the cotton mills, and Jackie got a job delivering bobbin spools to the weavers. She worked twelve hours a night for 6¢ an hour. When she was 9, Jackie was promoted to inspection room supervisor. One night a male foreman made an advance toward her. She hit the man hard on the nose; she was neither fired nor bothered again.

At the age of 11, Jackie moved into the home of a woman who owned three beauty shops. She learned to mix shampoos, color hair, and give permanent waves. She stayed there for about four years and then she made a series of moves: first to Montgomery, Alabama, where she worked as a beautician and trained to be a nurse but did not graduate because she knew she could not pass the written exam. Then she went back to Sawdust Road to help a country doctor; next to Pensacola, Florida, where she became co-owner of a beauty shop; then a brief stay in Mississippi; and finally back to Pensacola. It was here that she gave herself a new name, picking "Cochran" out of a phone book because she liked its sound.

In 1929, Jackie sold her interest in the beauty shop and headed for New York City, where she got a job at a hair salon on Fifth Avenue. The salon owner had another shop in Miami, Florida, and Jackie would follow her customers when they wintered in that city. At a dinner party in Miami, she met Floyd Odlum, a lawyer who also ran an investment firm. Jackie confided to Floyd that she wanted to sell cosmetics. He told her that if she planned to sell over a large area, she needed to learn to fly and advised her to get her pilot's license.

When Jackie returned to New York, she decided to use her vacation time to take flying lessons and enrolled in a flying school on Long Island. At that time, getting a license required twenty flying hours and passing a written examination. She took an oral exam instead. At the end of three weeks, Jackie had her pilot's license.

She knew she needed more training, so in 1933 Jackie went to a flying school in San Diego, California. She bought a used plane and practiced flight maneuvers and spot landings. It was a trial-and-error process. Because she could not write well, she hired a tutor to help her pass ground school instruction. After just six months' training, Jackie received her commercial pilot's license. Now it was time to spread her wings.

First Jackie joined an air circus in New York, flying acrobatics. While doing a show in Buffalo, she went into a terrible spin, recovering less than 500 feet above the ground. In another incident, she was piloting Floyd from New York to Miami when she ran into severe weather over South Carolina. For forty minutes, she flew blind. When she saw a clear patch of sky, she set the plane down in a cow pasture. She made up her mind to learn how to fly by looking at the plane's instruments instead of using the horizon and the earth as reference points. Jackie hired an expert in instrument flying to instruct her.

In 1934 she entered the MacRobertson London-to-Australia race. The 12,000-mile race had a $75,000 purse. Jackie had a bul-

let-shaped Northrop Gamma plane, called a *Gee Bee*. The
Northrop plane company cut the single cockpit and squeezed in
another seat for a copilot. They also installed an extra gas tank
that enabled the plane to fly 3,000 miles before refueling. It was
still being assembled when Jackie bought it over the phone; the
first time she saw the plane was when she arrived in London. The
Gee Bee was the fastest plane in the group, but winning the race
called for more than speed.

Jackie and her male copilot took off. They flew at 14,000 feet
with no oxygen; the plane was cold and noisy. As they tried to set
down in Bucharest, Hungary, trouble developed with the wing
flaps: one flap went down, but the other flap remained up, making it impossible to land. They made several passes at the runway.
Then the copilot wrote a note saying he wanted to bail out. Jackie
scribbled back that he could bail out if he wanted, but this was
her plane and she would stay with it. The copilot wrote, "You're a
fool," but he stayed with her.[7]

Finally the flaps went down. The plane landed hard and kept
going the entire length of the runway. When it stopped, the copilot quickly jumped out. Jackie took off her flying suit, applied lip-
stick, and combed her hair before leaving the plane. The groom-
ing became her postflight ritual. Several hours were needed to fix
the wing flaps, and it was not possible to make up the lost time.
Jackie Cochran's first race was over.

In 1935, Jackie decided to enter the Bendix Transcontinental
Air Race from Burbank, California to Cleveland, Ohio. Amelia
Earhart had been the first woman to fly this speed race in 1933,
and she was also an entrant in 1935. The race started at midnight
in order to avoid the morning fog and also because the engines
ran better in the cool night air.

Amelia Earhart took off, then unexpected fog rolled in. The
manufacturer of Jackie's plane did not want her to take it up
because the plane that took off before hers had exploded. She

made a phone call to Floyd, seeking his advice. He told her that there was a fine line between a course of action determined by logic and one dictated by great emotional urge. No one could dictate that course of action for anyone else. Jackie climbed back into her plane and took off. At dawn, the plane's tail started to vibrate violently and the engine overheated. She had to turn back to Los Angeles. Amelia Earhart placed fifth in the race.

Jackie first met Amelia Earhart in 1935. She liked the famous flier instantly, not only because of her accomplishments in aviation, but also because of her character. The two women could not have been more different: Amelia had a shy, gentle nature while Jackie was outspoken and aggressive. But they shared an obsessive love of flying and an appreciation of each other's aviation skills.

Amelia Earhart's first attempt to fly around the world was aborted when she had an accident in Hawaii. She discussed her second global trip with Jackie and Floyd in 1937. They were apprehensive, but they agreed to finance a portion of the trip. Amelia changed her original flight plan and decided to begin from Florida. Before she left in June 1937, Amelia gave Jackie a small, silk American flag. When Amelia failed to make her scheduled stop at Howland Island in the Pacific, search planes crisscrossed the ocean. Jackie and the entire nation mourned when the dreaded announcement came that Amelia could not be found. America had lost its most famous woman pilot—and Jackie had lost a friend.

In addition to a career in aviation, Cochran also had her own cosmetics business. In 1935, she started her company, Jacqueline Cochran's Cosmetics, Inc. with headquarters in New York City. Along with Dorothy Gray, Helena Rubinstein, and Elizabeth Arden, she founded the American cosmetics industry in the 1930s. In addition to her beauty products for women, she also developed a line of cosmetics for men. One item was a lip mois-

Jacqueline Cochran, director of the Women Airforce Service
Pilots, in her Pentagon office in Washington, D.C. She used her
personal influence and political skills to advance the cause of
the civilian women pilots within the Army Air Forces. *Courtesy of
The Woman's Collection, Texas Woman's University*

turizer in stick form, popular with pilots bothered by dry,
chapped lips.

Jacqueline Cochran was a walking advertisement for her
products. She had porcelain-like skin and huge brown eyes. Her
hands were large and she wore no nail polish on them. She wore
beautiful tailored suits and designer dresses, and she owned
many pairs of shoes. Jackie never believed beauty was incompati-

ble with accomplishment. She even had her company slogan, "WINGS TO BEAUTY," painted on the side of her plane.

In 1936 Jackie married Floyd Odlum. But she kept her name, Jacqueline Cochran, for personal and professional reasons. Floyd was fourteen years her senior and one of the wealthiest men in the United States. He financed her cosmetic business and her flying ventures. Floyd was interested in aviation and he lived this interest vicariously through his wife; he often helped Jackie plan her flights. He was stricken with severe arthritis shortly after their marriage so he could not travel with Jackie, but they spoke daily on the phone. Although the two had different temperaments, they shared the same goals: an appreciation of money, power, and fame, and a willingness to work incredibly hard to obtain these things. Their forty-year marriage was one of mutual admiration. Jackie spoke of her husband's kindness and generosity often. Floyd said simply, "My wife is the most interesting person I have ever met."[8]

In September 1937, Jackie entered the Bendix Race again. She placed third and was the only female pilot in the event. Then she won the New York-to-Miami speed race in four hours and twelve minutes, setting a national record. She had calculated her fuel so carefully that when she touched down in Miami, the gas tank was completely empty. That same year, Jackie became the first woman to make an instrument-only landing. She was also honored with the Harmon International Trophy—the first of fifteen—as the outstanding female pilot of the world.

For the 1938 Bendix Race, Jackie's new aircraft was a military pursuit, or fighter, plane. The P-35 had extra fuel tanks built into the wings so the trip could be made nonstop. She studied the plane's instrument panel for hours; then she worked blindfolded so she could operate by touch.

On the day of the race, Jackie was the only woman among the ten qualifying pilots. After she was aloft, bad weather closed in. She climbed to 22,000 feet, sucking on a tube connected to an oxygen canister. When she descended to 20,000 feet, the engine quit. She switched to the other gas tank. No result. Then she tipped the wing, and the engine started. She flew the remainder of the race, rocking the plane back and forth so fuel would flow to the tank.

The next afternoon in Cleveland, a huge crowd cheered as the first plane raced across the finish line. And from the cockpit, the winner emerged—with fresh makeup. Jacqueline Cochran had flown 2,042 miles in eight hours, ten minutes, and thirty-one seconds. She had less than three gallons of fuel in her tank. When mechanics inspected Jackie's plane, they found a wad of paper in the gas drainage valve that had been accidentally left when the gas tanks were installed at the factory.

Jackie climbed back into her plane and flew to Bendix Field, New Jersey. She set a new women's cross-country record by flying the total distance from California in ten hours, seven minutes, and ten seconds. The next day, she boarded a commercial airliner back to Cleveland to claim the Bendix trophy.

In 1939 she set a women's altitude record by flying 33,000 feet above sea level—over 6 miles high, the standard for today's passenger jets. The cockpit was not pressurized, and the temperature was -60° F. Jackie had no oxygen mask, relying on a tube from an oxygen canister. As she descended, a blood vessel ruptured in her sinus cavity. Light-headed and disoriented, she circled the airport for an hour before landing. The next day, she received word she had won her second Harmon Trophy.

There were many other harrowing moments in Jackie Cochran's aviation career. On one trip, the fuel line ruptured inside the plane, soaking her with gasoline. She sat in the cockpit knowing a single spark would result in a fiery death. But she did not panic and brought the plane in for a smooth landing. Before the plane came to a complete stop, she jumped out and stripped off her wet flying suit.

Jacqueline Cochran was known as a fearless pilot because of the risks she took. She refused to let fear steal her nerve and she minimized risks by careful planning. She studied her planes, maps, the weather—the many details that go into piloting. Before a major race, she trained like an athlete with exercises, a high-protein diet, and pep talks to herself. But she was also superstitious. On the sides of her planes, she painted the number thirteen, which she believed brought her good luck.

Yet no amount of calculation could prepare for the unforeseen: a sudden shift of weather, mechanical failure. Jackie knew accidents and death could happen. But, she said, "If you ponder such possibilities too long or too often, you'll never risk anything. And to live without risk for me would have been tantamount to death."[9]

FOUR

Fighting for the Right to Fly

We are the feminine reality
Of flight dreams that have long been unfulfilled.

—44-W-2 YEARBOOK

In September 1939, a few weeks after Germany invaded Poland—
the horrible beginning of World War II—Jackie wrote a letter to
First Lady Eleanor Roosevelt about the possibility of using women
pilots if the United States went to war. Mrs. Roosevelt was
intrigued and mentioned the aviator's idea in her newspaper col-
umn, "My Day."

Jackie believed women made excellent pilots. She thought
they had more patience and possessed a better sense of detail
than men did. However, she had few close female friends. By her
own admission, she preferred the company of men. She aroused
controversy among the other women pilots, and many did not
like her. But her detractors acknowledged her achievements in
aviation and believed in her vision for women pilots.

In June 1941, Jackie met with a recruiter for the British Ferry
Command and also with Henry H. "Hap" Arnold, commanding

general of the U.S. Army Air Corps. Although Great Britain used its women pilots to ferry planes from the factories to air fields, its need for pilots was so great that they sought assistance from other countries. General Arnold asked Jackie if she would like to fly a Lockheed *Hudson,* a British bomber, to Scotland to dramatize Great Britain's need for help. She leaped at the chance to become the first American woman to fly a bomber, even though she had no experience with the heavy plane.

Jackie set about learning to fly the bomber. After twenty-five flying hours, she went to Montreal for her check rides, a series of tests which determined if certain flying skills were mastered. She passed these but faced objections from the male ferry pilots. Some resented the publicity, while others thought she could not fly the heavy plane. Officials reached a compromise that would pacify the men. She could fly the bomber across the Atlantic, but had to relinquish the controls to her male copilot on takeoff and landing.

In England, Jackie met with the head of the women's ferrying auxiliary, Pauline Glower, who asked her to recruit American female pilots. The day after her return, she was summoned to the White House where she gave a report to President and Mrs. Roosevelt. The president asked Jackie to research how women pilots could be used in the United States. She was to work with General Arnold and Col. Robert Olds, head of the Ferry Command.

For a month Jackie and her business staff went through papers of the Civil Aeronautical Administration, which kept records of all licensed pilots in the United States. She found 3,000 licensed female pilots. She wrote letters to 150 commercially licensed women pilots who had over 200 flying hours each. She asked if they were interested in flying military aircraft; 130 responded yes. She drew up a plan, which formed the basis of her later training program, the Women's Flying Training Detachment (WFTD).

Her plan called for military training of women who held private pilots' licenses. They would deliver military planes from the factories to air bases and port cities within the continental United States. She also proposed that these women be limited to non-combat roles, unlike the Soviet female fighter pilots—called the "night witches"—who gained a fearsome reputation for their night bombing raids against the Germans.

Jackie wrote her report and submitted it to Colonel Olds and General Arnold. They rejected it. Colonel Olds wanted a smaller, limited program. General Arnold thought the all-female pilot program would arouse controversy within the military and was not needed at the time.

Jackie went back to New York and began recruiting women for the British war effort. She took twenty-five women pilots to England where they trained with the Royal Air Force. These women served with the British Air Transport Auxiliary (ATA), moving planes from factories to bases. They were called the "ATA Girls." During their eighteen months of work, only one American pilot died when the propeller flew off her plane.

Jackie was still in England when a pivotal—and horrible—event took place, December 7, 1941. On a clear Sunday morning in Honolulu, Hawaii, a group of small, swift Japanese planes, each painted with a picture of the rising sun, flew over the mountains and dropped their bombs on the American fleet in Pearl Harbor. The following day, President Roosevelt asked Congress to declare war on Japan. The United States joined the Allied forces: Great Britain, France, and Russia. America was now fully involved in this global war.

Military bases sprang up throughout the country to train soldiers, sailors, and pilots. Munitions, ship, and aircraft factories ran around the clock. Women left their kitchens to work in the factories and coined for themselves a new name, "Rosie the Riveter." The United States threw its mighty collective energy into fighting World War II. The military would have to call on the women pilots—and they gladly responded.

Jackie Cochran was not the only person who had the idea of using women pilots in the war. Another notable American female aviator, Nancy Harkness Love, had also drawn up a plan. Like Cochran, she would limit civilian women pilots to noncombat roles and flying within the continental United States. However, her women pilots had to meet higher criteria: hold a commercial pilot's license; have a minimum of 500 flying hours; and have experience in cross-country flying. Because of extensive flying experience, they would need only transitional training before they could fly military planes.

Nancy Love's proposal was approved within the Army Air Forces. This group of women pilots, activated in September 1942, was called the Women's Auxiliary Ferry Squadron (WAFS). There were forty-nine women pilots in the United States who could meet Nancy Love's standards; she picked twenty-five. These WAFS averaged over 1,100 flying hours.

Jackie Cochran was furious when she heard about the WAFS. She stormed into General Arnold's office and argued for her larger training program until he gave in. Jackie Cochran would have her group. It was named the Women's Flying Training Detachment (WFTD), with Jackie as director. She offered to do this job for $1 a year because she believed in the program and wanted to command it. In August 1943, the two civilian women groups merged into one organization, renamed the Women Airforce Service Pilots (WASP) with Jackie Cochran as director. Love was still in charge of the women pilots in the Ferrying Division, but she served under Jackie's command.

The WASP remained a civilian and auxiliary program. It was attached *to* the Army Air Forces, but the women were not members *of* the military. As a civilian organization, the women's pilot training program was put into place quickly—waiting for congressional approval to grant military status would have taken too much time. Being civilian meant that WASPs were not eligible for military privileges such as insurance and death benefits. But Jackie Cochran's intent was to get military status for the WASP: That battle would soon come. And it would affect 44-W-2 profoundly.

The years 1942-44 were hectic for Jackie Cochran. In addition to her women's pilot training program, she had a cosmetics empire to run and a husband she rarely saw. Her travel schedule was horrendous, shuttling between Washington, D.C., Sweetwater, and the various bases where the WASPs served. How did she do it? She juggled. And she hired the best people to help. She said of those days, "It was all happening too fast, even for me. My worries were overwhelming. Without chief administrative officer Leni Leoti Deaton, I would have drowned."[10]

And she persisted. She fought for this program. She was told no, women were not needed; no, women were not capable of flying military aircraft; no, it could not be done. Jackie Cochran never heard a "no" she liked. This former child of poverty was not stopped by a mere word. She went over, under, and around a no—or she met it head on.

So it was with great pride that Miss Jacqueline Cochran, Director of Women Airforce Service Pilots, handed silver-winged pins to her latest graduates at Avenger Field that warm September 1943 morning. Marie Michell and the class of 44-W-2 would walk across the same platform the following March to receive their wings and diplomas. It would be an exciting—and grueling—six months.

FIVE

Up in the Air

*Once you have flown an airplane, your world is never
the same again.*

—JEAN HASCALL COLE, WASP 44-W-2

By October 1943, Marie Michell was sky high into primary training. She and her classmates had to successfully complete fifty-five flying hours in their primary trainer plane, the PT-19A. Civilian instructors gave training on aerial maneuvers and checked the skills mastered. In addition, Avenger trainees were checked by military pilots assigned to the base. Marie and the rest of 44-W-2 had mastered most of the basic maneuvers when they earned their private pilots' licenses. However, they had to prove they could perform these skills in the heavier military planes.

Primary training took place at auxiliary fields, only a few miles from Avenger Field. Trainees rode to and from those fields in the cattle trucks. As they bounced along, they sang some of the many WASP songs. One of their favorites was "Ready But Right." But they were warned not to sing the risqué lyrics if Jackie Cochran was on the base.

An Avenger Field trainee ready to board a PT-13 *Kaydet*. **Produced by Stearman, a division of Boeing, this primary trainer was a tandem two-seater with an open cockpit and had a maximum speed level of 124 mph.** *Courtesy of The Woman's Collection, Texas Woman's University*

After they arrived at the field's "ready room," instructors gave them general flight information and directions. Outside, they could see their training planes. The PT-19A was a single-engine plane with an open dual cockpit and low, fabric-covered wings. The whole plane was covered with several layers of silver paint. With a 175-horsepower engine, the PT-19A was the largest and most powerful plane many had ever flown.

The aircraft also had dual controls. The instructor sat in the cockpit directly behind the trainee and initially operated the control stick from the back. As the trainee progressed, control was gradually relinquished to the pilot. The instructor had a microphone which connected to headphones in the front cockpit; instructions were given through a one-way speaking tube called a gosport.

Most of the civilian flight instructors liked their jobs and enjoyed working with the trainees. And most student pilots liked their instructors.

But there were exceptions. One instructor failed all his trainees before he was transferred from Avenger Field. Another instructor was abusive. The man would shove his control stick rapidly back and forth, causing the trainee's control stick to hit the inside of her knees. His students often bore black-and-blue bruises on their legs. He also yelled profanities at them, and if the student did not do something he wanted, he took the earphones and held them over the side of the plane. The sound of the rushing wind whipped right into the trainee's ears. In spite of this abuse, all his trainees stuck it out and graduated.

One of the first flight procedures the women learned on the PT-19A was to take off, maintain a level flight, climb, turn, and glide. And because most accidents happen when planes go into stalls and spins, trainees were taught what to do if this occurred. They practiced deliberately stalling the plane by pulling the stick all the way back. This put the plane into a steep climb until its nose began to drop and it went into a downward spiral. To recover from the spin, the trainee pushed or "popped" the stick forward until the plane leveled. During a spin, the pilot's head would whiplash around. Then the women understood why Lieutenant LaRue made them do endless head rolls in exercise class to strengthen their neck muscles.

They also practiced aerial slow rolls, snap rolls, figure eights, and other maneuvers. And of course, they practiced landings, which were—and still are—the most perilous part of flying. Since there was no radio in the primary trainer to communicate with the flight tower, the pilot relied on tower lights to tell her when to land. A green light indicated the pilot was cleared for landing; a red light meant she was not, in which case she circled until she got a green light.

After eight hours of dual flying, or about a week, the student was ready to solo. She went through the maneuvers called by the instructor in the backseat. After the solo, she waited anxiously with her baymates in the ready room to learn if she had passed. The first ones to solo in each flight were dumped by their baymates in the Wishing Well, an above-ground stone well. They scooped up coins from the bottom of the well for their baymates.

After every landing, each student had to record the amount of flight time in her pilot's logbook. She received demerits if she failed to keep proper flight records. To avoid this, she would attach a strip of masking tape above one knee of her zoot suit and record her flying time before she took off and after she landed. When she went back to the ready room, she transferred the numbers to her logbook.

Even though Avenger Field had over 300 flying days a year, weather was always a factor, particularly when sandstorms—called "Texas rain"—came boiling out of the west-southwest. When the red clouds appeared on the horizon, smoke pots were put out at the auxiliary fields to call off flying. If pilots were in the air, they would see the smoke and come in before the dust storm hit. The maintenance crews hurried to tie down the planes and place covers over the engines and propellers.

When a sandstorm hit, visibility dropped to zero. Sometimes the dust blew for hours, darkening the sun. People tied wet cloths around their faces to keep from breathing the choking dust. Grains of sand hitting the body felt like needles. Skin took on the texture of stucco, and everyone walked around with goggle and helmet tans.

Every time the trainees finished flying, they brought back stories to their baymates. One that made the rounds was about Pat Church's surprise snake. One morning, Pat was in the air with her instructor. Unknown to them, a snake had crawled into the hollow wing through a small hole in the seam of the fabric. Sometime during takeoff or ascent, the snake was so disturbed that it came crawling out on top of the wing. Pat and her instructor could only stare at the snake inching toward the cockpit. Luckily the force of the wind gradually pushed the snake off the plane and it dropped to the earth.

Other incidents were more dangerous. One trainee went up by herself to practice spins, and in the excitement, forgot to fasten her seat belt. She pushed the stick forward to come out of her spin, when she suddenly flew out of her seat and landed on top of the plane. Fortunately, at that moment, the plane straightened out, and she was thrown back into her seat. She never forgot to fasten her seat belt again.

The military pilots at Avenger Field did the flight checks that would determine whether the trainees passed and went on to the next level or washed out. The period of days prior to military checks was a time of extreme anxiety. The women had difficulty eating or sleeping, a condition known as "checkitis." Before the trainee went on her check ride, she tossed a coin in the Wishing Well for good luck.

On the day of the flight check, the military pilot sat in the back seat and gave instructions through the gosport to the student in front. She had to do takeoffs, spins, stalls, landings, forced landings, and other maneuvers. The check pilot gave an "S" for satisfactory performance and a "U" for unsatisfactory. If a trainee received a "U," she got another chance. If she failed her second check ride, she got a pink paper slip: She had washed out of the WASP program and had to pay her way back home.

Most of the washouts took place during the primary training phase. Much to their chagrin, 44-W-2 had a higher washout rate than many other classes. Years later when class members gathered, they speculated about the reasons: a beefed-up curriculum; personality clashes between some trainees and their instructors; a larger number of younger, inexperienced trainees in the class; or perhaps the military was trying to eliminate as many women pilots as possible.

This trainee was dunked in the Wishing Well after a successful solo. Money in the bottom of the well came from the women tossing coins to wish for good luck in passing courses or the military check ride. *Courtesy of The Woman's Collection, Texas Woman's University*

And why did those that remained not wash out? Maybe it was an overwhelming desire to fly and a willingness to put up with most anything to do so. And surely stubbornness, a tough mental attitude, and a trainee's belief in herself that she would not fail. Or maybe luck—or all of these things.

When the members of 44-W-2 were not in flight, they were in ground school or in calisthenics. Included in the physical training was close-order drill conducted by Lieutenant LaRue: straight lines, taller women in the back, chins up, a stiff-armed swing. Led by their own section leader, they marched everywhere: to mess hall, flight line, physical training, ground school. As they marched, they sang songs passed on by upperclasswomen, and they made up their own lyrics to existing tunes. Deedie Deaton called Avenger Field the "singing base."

The curriculum in ground school was tough, particularly for the younger trainees who had little or no college education. After the evening meal, the older women with college degrees helped the younger—and each other—through the challenging courses that involved physics and higher mathematics.

Morse code was difficult for everyone. In October 1942, the Army Air Forces changed the curriculum, requiring male and female pilot cadets to send and receive ten words per minute, up from six words per minute. Even after a trainee completed the Morse code requirements, she had to return every week to pass another test. If she failed, she returned to regular ground school class until she passed.

In spite of—or perhaps because of—the pressure, trainees added some humor to the program. Flight One had fun with their meteorology instructor. The group wore dark glasses inside the classroom. One person would cross her legs, which was a signal for the others to reach up and move their glasses slightly off-center. Soon, the instructor listed in the direction of the tilted glasses. After a while, another person would cross her legs in the opposite direction, and everyone would adjust their glasses off-kilter to the other side. And the instructor leaned in that direction. So it continued—right, left, right, left—it drove the man crazy, and as far as anyone knew, he never caught on to the trick.

Saturday morning was inspection time. Everyone was up early to get everything in spic-and-span order. Articles had to be stowed neatly in the closets or footlockers. Shoes had to be placed under the bed with toes pointing out. And not a speck of dust was tolerated, in spite of the fact that the wind deposited mini sand dunes on the window sills. The women polished the floor by slipping on their zoot suits and sliding around the floor until it shone. Dusting might have been easier, but this was more fun!

The beds had to be made just-so: sheets turned down two hands' width over the blankets; blankets tight enough to bounce coins on. Trainees crawled under their beds and tied sheets and blankets to get them taut. The upperclasswomen called 44-W-2 "eager beavers," which was true the first two weeks. By the third week, they were trying to see how much they could get away with.

Saturday afternoons and Sundays were free time unless bad weather during the week had cut into flying time, in which case they were in the air those days. For fun, the women went into Sweetwater, where they shopped at Levy's department store or Sears and Roebuck. Or they had soft drinks at the Bluebonnet drugstore. On Saturday nights, the cattle trucks carried them to the Avengerette, the women's clubhouse in Sweetwater. Men came from bases in Abilene and Big Spring. The party-goers played records and danced. Some drank.

In spite of the strict rule of no alcohol on base, the women hated to leave partially consumed bottles behind. So they took the liquor back to base. Mrs. Deaton was wise to the hiding places and made periodic checks of lockers and bathrooms. But 44-W-2 buried their bottles in the dirt space between barracks, marking the place with sticks. Over Saturday nights, small cemeteries of liquor bottles would spring up between the barracks.

For trainees, Sunday was the only day their lives were not scheduled to the minute and most slept late. Some spent the day writing letters, studying, or washing hair or clothes. Two women had brought their cars with them. Sometimes they piled baymates into their cars and drove to Lake Sweetwater, where they swam and sunbathed.

During the first week of October, only a month into training, word went around Avenger Field that a WASP graduate had been killed. Virginia Moffatt, class 43-W-2, had been assigned to the Sixth Ferry Group at Long Beach, California. On October 5, she was killed while landing a BT-15, a basic trainer plane. The cause was undetermined. Virginia was a skilled pilot, fully capable of making a routine landing in a plane that was not difficult to fly.

Sixteen-hour training days left little time for relaxing, except on weekends. These trainees used chairs from their rooms to make themselves more comfortable while spending their day off sunbathing between their barracks at Avenger Field. *Courtesy of The Woman's Collection, Texas Woman's University*

Because she was a civilian pilot, her family could not receive military death benefits nor would the military supply an American flag to cover her coffin. The WASPs at Long Beach took up a collection to pay for the costs of shipping her body by train to her home in Los Angeles.

Marie Michell and Kit MacKethan, who were in Flight Two together, made a lighthearted pledge to each other. If one were killed, the other would go to be with the grieving mother. It was a pledge neither expected to have to fulfill.

SIX

Bucket of Bolts and the Hood

You sat up there, and God was right there with you.

—EVELYN GREENBLATT HOWREN, WASP 43-W-1

In November 1943, Marie and her classmates started their intermediate training amid constant war news. In the European theater, Allied bombers pounded Berlin, Germany, and in the
Pacific, seventy-two Japanese planes were downed in the Marshall
Islands. That same month, American aviation factories produced
1,000 four-engine bombers and 7,789 other types of aircraft. As
quickly and professionally as possible, Avenger Field trained its
women pilots to deliver these aircraft where they were needed
within the United States.

Intermediate training included two phases of instrument flying. The first phase meant about twenty hours in the "blue box,"
a Link trainer that taught instrument flying; the second half was
actually flying by instruments. Trainees also had to pass their two
check flights on the basic and advanced trainer planes. The first
aircraft they had to master was the BT-13 (or the BT-15, a similar
basic trainer), which they called the "Bucket of Bolts," the "Vultee

Vibrator," and a few unprintable names. The BT-13 had a 440-horsepower engine, fixed landing gear, and a closed dual cockpit. It was sleek shaped and murder to fly. The typical BT-13 at Avenger was old, it rattled and shook, the radio reception was poor, and each plane handled differently. But worst of all, the plane was unpredictable in spins.

Lorraine Zillner, in Flight Two, had a frightening experience in her BT-15. She was flying alone when the plane suddenly flipped over and went into an inverted spin. She tried everything she had been taught to bring the plane out of the spin. As the plane spiraled ever closer to the ground, she was forced to bail out. But she had difficulty getting out because she was in an inverted position. Lorraine struggled to free herself and finally fell out of the plane. One leg hit the rudder. With the ground fast approaching, she yanked the rip cord on her parachute. No counting from one to ten—just one, ten. The chute opened just before she hit the ground.

As Lorraine lay dazed in the middle of a cotton field, two cowboys rode up. One pulled off her helmet and exclaimed, "My gosh, it's a little girl."

Lorraine started to cry. One cowboy tried to comfort her, while the other came back with a branch of cotton to dry her eyes. He said, "Here, don't cry, don't cry. We'll get help."[11]

But help was already on the way. Kit MacKethan saw the plane crash but did not see the parachute open. She radioed Avenger Field, and they sent an ambulance. Lorraine clutched her rip cord all the way back to base. Her injured leg was bandaged, and she spent one night in the infirmary. Two days later, she was back in the air again.

Lorraine sought out the civilian worker responsible for packing parachutes to thank her for her care and diligence. She also wrote the manufacturer, telling the company it made "a darn good parachute." She became an automatic member of the

Caterpillar Club, a select group of fall survivors. As a memento, she kept her rip cord. It was one of her most prized possessions.

In spite of the BT's drawbacks, trainees soloed after about a week of training. After another week of basic maneuvers, everyone moved on to the AT-6, the advanced trainer. The AT-6 *Texan*—also called the "Sweet Six"—was a dream plane. It had a 600-horsepower engine, retractable landing gear, and a covered dual cockpit. The plane was easy to handle and extremely responsive in maneuvers.

About the same time 44-W-2 moved up to the AT-6, they also began Link, for instrument training. The Link program was used to teach all military and commercial pilots how to fly at night or during bad weather by using the plane's instrument panel.

Each Link trainer looked like a miniature airplane with a covered cockpit. The trainee was shut into the Link for an hour or so of instruction. Inside, the student sat before an airplane instrument panel. She had controls to operate and a chart to consult. The instructor sat outside and had a similar but larger chart spread on a big table. The instructor gave directions by radio. As the trainee "flew," her reactions were recorded on the outside chart by a large stylus. At the end of the lesson, the operator showed the student what mistakes she had made and whether she had arrived at the correct destination.

In the Link, the student had to fly by radio beam—a technique called "flying the beam"—to land in the right place. In the 1940s, the United States was crisscrossed with radio stations, each having its own frequency and beams. Some of the sending stations were located at or near local airports. Every station had a different Morse code to identify its location.

For example, to locate Cleveland, Ohio by instruments, the student found the Morse code for the Cleveland beacon on her map and tuned into the radio frequency as she approached the city. If she correctly tuned her receiver, she heard the sounds of

Link planes had aircraft instruments and controls that simulated flying. Trainees had to complete twenty to thirty hours of Link training before actually flying by instruments. *Courtesy of The Woman's Collection, Texas Woman's University*

dot-dash (Morse code for the letter A) and dash-dot (letter N) which overlapped to produce a steady hum. She was now flying "on the beam." If she were flying away from Cleveland, the hum grew fainter; if she were flying toward the airport, the hum grew louder as she approached. When she heard no sound, that meant she was right over the Cleveland airport. She had entered the "cone of silence." Had this cone-shaped area been visible, it would have become larger as it rose; thus, no matter how high the plane was, the pilot hit silence if she were over the correct destination.

At this point, the trainee could begin her descent. If she had calculated her altitude correctly with her airspeed, she saw the Cleveland runway below her plane when she broke through to clear sky. If she could not find the runway and attempted to land, she "crashed." Wreaths were hung on the Link room walls in memory of those who had "died" during Link training. In reality, before that happened, the trainee was allowed to see the mistakes she was making. Link was intense, frustrating claustrophobic work. But it was absolutely necessary for trainees to master Morse code and instrument training before going on to the real thing.

Marie Michell breezed through Link training because she had been a Link instructor prior to arriving at Avenger. Although she was nineteen at the time, Marie's experience as a Link operator helped to get her accepted into the pilot training program. Her good friend, Kit MacKethan, had also been a Link instructor in Atlanta, Georgia.

December was a busy month for Avenger trainees. The last class of the year, 43-W-8, graduated and the base prepared for Christmas celebrations. The Avenger chorus met on Tuesday and Thursday evenings to rehearse holiday selections. Mrs. Deaton ordered a 12 ft. Christmas tree for the gym, and trainees decorated their own bays. A Christmas Eve party was planned in the gym. All leaves were cancelled during the holiday, but trainees could invite dates to the party.

As the celebrants entered the gym on Christmas Eve, the piano was playing and mistletoe hung everywhere. Invited male cadet officers had on their dress uniforms. Avenger women dressed in suits or formal dresses. The band played dance music, and winners were announced for the tango, rhumba, and jitterbug contests. Class flight members presented skits and Marie was the featured actor in her flight's skit. The Avenger chorus also sang Christmas carols. At midnight, Santa arrived with gift bags for trainees and guests. And appropriately, it started to snow.

On Christmas Day, some of the women had dinner with civilian instructors and their families, and a few accepted invitations from Sweetwater citizens. But most trainees elected to spend

Christmas with classmates and to eat dinner in the mess hall. This was when the famous "Beatrice" incident occurred.

Lorraine Zillner's parents did not want their daughter to spend Christmas without family so they sent her brother, Bud, to visit from Illinois. One of Lorraine's baymates was called home because of serious illness in her family. To save on hotel costs and because there was an available bed, Lorraine sneaked Bud into her bay for the remainder of his stay. Baymates dressed him in a zoot suit, put a white turban on his head, and introduced him as Beatrice. He went with them to ground school and mess hall. Before nightly bed checks, they hid him in the next bay, and then ran him back when the checker left. While he showered and dressed, someone kept watch outside the bathroom door.

Beatrice was a great joke, and one that only Flight Two knew—or so they thought. Years later at a WASP reunion, Mrs. Deaton approached Lorraine and asked about Beatrice. Startled, Lorraine replied that Beatrice was fine. Then Mrs. Deaton told Lorraine that she and her staff had known all along that Beatrice was really her brother, but they decided to let him stay because he had come so far to be with her at Christmas.

The snow that started on Christmas Eve 1943 continued. Trainees played in the snow and took pictures. The temperature plunged, icicles hung from the eaves, and the wind piled snow into 2 ft. drifts. Planes were grounded and leaves were cancelled. The ground froze like concrete in the liquor-bottle cemetery, leaving trainees chopping away in futility. Then the main gas line broke. The only heat at Avenger came from two fireplaces, one of which was in Mrs. Deaton's office. Marie and friends put on their long underwear, heavy gym suits, and fleece-lined leather flight suits when they went to bed.

The new year, 1944, brought new snow. The wind swept the prairies clean and deposited snow on the runways, which were packed solid. Flight training resumed, and instructors were subject to savage snowball attacks. The class of 44-W-2 advanced from Link training to real flights based on instruments only. To fly "under the hood," students used a BT-15. The pilot sat in the front cockpit, which had a black accordian-pleated cover under the cockpit canopy. She could not see out and had to use her instrument panel to fly. The instructor sat in the back cockpit and gave instructions through the headphones. He could also take over the plane if the trainee got into trouble. The student had to fly under the hood to Abilene or Big Spring, find the beam, and land at these places. Then she flew back to Avenger the same way.

After a trainee passed her military check rides on instruments, she was teamed with a flightmate, or "buddy." One person would fly under the hood, while the other sat in the back and watched out for other aircraft. Then they switched places. There was no instructor to bail them out of trouble. They learned to develop trust in each other's flying ability and literally put their lives in one another's hands.

Marie and classmates spent the last two weeks in January doing night flying in the AT-6. Flying in the dark gave them a chance to practice their instrument skills, and it also prepared them for the long cross-country flights they would take during advanced training. As night fell, trainees trooped to the canteen and picked up sandwiches and coffee as they waited for their turn to fly.

Jean Hascall in Flight One had a terrible experience during night flying. One evening as she was sleeping on a bench in the ready room, awaiting her turn to fly, her instructor came into the room and shoved her to the floor. She picked herself up and completed her flight. Later, during another flight, he flipped the plane suddenly in a violent maneuver. Jean struck her head and experienced a "red out." As blood rushed to her head, she lost consciousness. She awoke to her hands flapping and a voice coming in through her headphones, "Are you all right? Are you all right?"[12]

Jean was not all right. She was bleeding from her nose and eyes and was nauseated. The instructor flew the plane back in and told her to "write it up," meaning she should fill out the form to file for the flight. She did not want to wash out so she wrote, "All okay." She went back to her bay, crawled into bed, and told no one. She never knew the reasons why her instructor had treated her so badly and she never had another flight with him. However, she did not quit; she was determined to finish her training. Soon after, the instructor left Avenger Field.

Most students had problems with night flying. The light from the stars combined with the ground light caused disorientation; it was difficult for the trainees to get their bearings. Also the darkness distorted the sense of space and distance, and the ground seemed closer than it actually was. As a result, pilots had a tendency to try to land too soon and came in several feet over the runway below.

Although night flying was hazardous, it also had its beautiful moments. The trainees streaked down a runway lined with flares and lifted into the heavens. The black sky was all encompassing, all star twinkling. But during the last week in January, the moon showed her full face. And the landscape, which appeared so harsh in the daylight, now glowed with a lunar beauty. The pilots, free from earth's constraints, flew with silver-winged Artemis* across the night sky.

---

* Artemis was the Greek goddess of the moon. She was the twin of Apollo, god of the sun, and daughter of Zeus. She was also the protector of women.

SEVEN

Crossing the Country

Look at me.
I say
Look at me
Riding through eternity.

—ANNE NOGGLE, WASP 44-W-1

In mid-January 1944, Marie Michell and 44-W-2 began their last training phase: cross-country navigation which involved short, medium, and long-distance flight. For these trips, they had to use all the ground and flight skills they had been taught at Avenger. The purpose of these final seventy hours of flying was to prepare them for flying aircraft under many different conditions. They would need this cross-country experience to prepare them for the conditions they would encounter during their upcoming service.

As the women were sky high into advanced training, the issue of giving them military status came up. In truth, it had never gone away. From the time she conceived her civilian training program, Jackie Cochran intended to get her women pilots militarized, and she lobbied hard for this cause. In the spring of 1943, General Arnold offered to put Jackie's group into the Women's Army Corps (WAC), where they would be granted military status.

Jackie flatly refused to consider this option. She argued that her pilots were different from the other women who served in the army. She also would have to be under the command of the female head of the WAC, Oveta Culp Hobby. Jackie had created her program and she intended to keep it. The only other way that WASP could be militarized would involve Congress passing a bill which would establish and fund this special unit. General Arnold supported this political effort, but he and Jackie knew the risks were high.

On Valentine's Day, Jackie Cochran made a surprise visit to Avenger Field. She gave the trainees an update on the WASP militarization bill introduced in the House of Representatives. Representative John Costello of California had introduced bill H.R. 4219, which if passed, would confer military status on the WASPs.

About the same time, another bill granting certain rights to those already in the military had been submitted to Congress. This bill, which came to be known as the "G.I. Bill of Rights," contained the following provisions: a sum of money payable to veterans when they left the military, depending on time served; an allowance for veterans to pursue education or vocational training if honorably discharged; low-interest loans to purchase houses or farms; an allowance for unemployment; hospital care and rehabilitation for wounded or disabled veterans; and a new government agency, called the Veterans Administration, which would be responsible for handling all claims. The WASPs would not be eligible for any of these benefits unless they became an official part of the military.

Marie Michell and classmates were concerned about getting military status, of course, but their most immediate worry was suc-

The AT-6 *Texan* was an advanced trainer known as "the pilot maker." The plane was sold to many countries around the world and remained in use over forty years after it was introduced in the late 1930s. *Courtesy of The Woman's Collection, Texas Woman's University*

cessfully completing their long-distance flights without crashing or getting lost. Advanced cross-country training was divided into three parts: short cross-country, which was 200 to 500 miles; medium cross-country covered 500 to 1,000 miles; and the final and longest journey was about 2,000 miles from Avenger Field to Blythe Army Air Base in California. They flew both PT-19s and AT-6s on the shorter flights, and AT-6s on the last trip.

During their final cross-country trip to Blythe, the pilots flew only during daylight hours. They made overnight refueling stops in El Paso, Texas and Tucson, Arizona. Flight instructors flew ahead and waited for them at the next stop. For many trainees, the flight over the western United States was a new and wonderful experience. Lifting off and soaring over deserts and the Rocky Mountain range, they looked down upon the beauty of the American West. Each flight took off on the same day, but after they were airborne, every pilot was on her own.

Before leaving, each pilot carefully plotted her own way to California. She watched her topography for landmarks that were marked on her maps. Flying visually is called pilotage, and pilots of single engine planes still use this navigational system today. On the way to California, she also contacted the ground stations that were on the maps.

In spite of this, pilots did get lost. It happened to Verda-Mae Lowe in Flight One. She was soaring over desert country when she saw a huge irrigation ditch. She had never seen an irrigation ditch before and thought she had crossed a river and was too far south in Mexico. She turned around but ran into clouds and got lost. Verda-Mae prayed for divine deliverance. At that moment the clouds parted, and she saw a green field with a parade ground. Giving thanks, she set the plane down. It was then she saw people in the distance and they were Japanese. "My God," she thought. "I've overshot the Pacific. I'm a one-woman invasion of Tokyo."[13]

But Verda-Mae had not landed in Tokyo. Instead she had put down in an internment camp, a detention center where the United States government had imprisoned Japanese Americans for fear they posed a security threat to the United States during the war. Eventually, a military pilot flew the AT-6 and Verda-Mae out, but with great difficulty because of the additional weight of the second pilot.

Yvonne "Shorty" Stafford, Flight Two, also got lost flying cross-country. Heading back to Avenger, she got off course and landed in a Mexican sheep pasture. Although her plane looked like metal, it was really canvas that was stretched over the plane's frame and secured with an alcohol-based glue. Sheep were soon attracted by the smell of the glue and came to nibble at the airplane. This, of course, would have rendered the plane useless in flying. During training every pilot was told to save the plane, if possible, short of putting her life in danger. So Shorty picked up a stick and tried to herd the sheep away.

Presently, a Mexican cowboy came riding up. He spoke no English and Shorty spoke no Spanish. She did have a pencil and paper so she wrote a message saying she was all right. Through gestures, she made the rider understand that he must deliver the note to someone who knew English. The cowboy galloped away to a house about twenty miles distant. The man there had a Model-T Ford so he drove forty miles to the nearest phone. These events took place over several hours.

Back at Avenger, the commander was concerned when Shorty did not arrive at her scheduled time. It was standard base policy to notify the next of kin if a pilot was missing for a certain length of time. After a couple of hours, Major Urban asked Mrs. Deaton to notify Shorty's parents. Deedie resisted, knowing the panic and worry the news would cause. When Major Urban said it was a military directive that she call, Mrs. Deaton replied, "We're not military." [14]

So began the long wait for a call from or about the missing pilot. About 11:00 P.M., Deedie finally relented and placed a call to Shorty's parents. She told them that their daughter had not reported back from cross-country, but she was sure Shorty was all right and that she would let them know as soon as possible. Deedie had just hung up when Major Urban called with the news that Shorty was safe. He later told Mrs. Deaton that when the military pilots arrived at the pasture, they found Shorty still shooing sheep away from her plane. When Shorty later walked into Mrs. Deaton's office, Deedie looked up and said, "Baaa!"[15]

From that point on, wherever Shorty went—to mess hall, flight line, boarding the cattle truck, marching in formation— she was greeted with the sound of bleating sheep.

On February 22, 1944, Flight Two started for the final cross-country to California. Betty Pauline Stine was one of the first to take off. When they arrived in El Paso, Betty and her good friend, Fran Smith, made a visit over the border into Mexico where Betty bought a big straw hat and a bottle of wine. She did not have room in her plane for the items so Fran stowed them in her aircraft. The next day, they went on to Tucson for refueling and another stay overnight. A group of pursuit pilots was stationed at the base where they reported, and one of the P-38 pilots took a shine to Betty. He led the way over the mountains to Blythe. The two played tag with each other in the air.

On February 25, Betty and Fran left Blythe for the return trip. They had planned to fly back together. Fran took off first in her AT-6 and circled, waiting for Betty. Finally, she decided to go on alone because circling was consuming valuable fuel.

At 4:00 P.M., Betty lifted off. Almost immediately, she ran into bad weather over the mountains. Then suddenly flames shot out from her engine, and Betty bailed out. A violent burst of wind caught her parachute and slammed her into the side of a cliff, dragging her along the rocks. Horrified and helpless, miners in the area witnessed the accident. Rescuers scrambled to the site, located Betty, and carried her badly injured body to a waiting ambulance. They rushed her to Blythe Army Air Base hospital where she died of massive head injuries.

Military officials made calls to Avenger Field and—the saddest one of all—to her parents. A second round of 44-W-2 trainees flew into Blythe while Mr. and Mrs. Stine were there to claim the body. In the group was Betty's other close friend, Mary Strok. The weeping parents told her that Betty had been killed.

Others in Flight Two learned about Betty's death in Tucson, where they were waiting for bad weather to blow over. Some did not know until they returned to Avenger Field. Those in Flight One heard about Betty before they left for California. They had to take the same route and they flew with foreboding and great caution. After Betty's accident, all trainees had to fly with a buddy, keeping within sight of each other's plane.

She was the lone person in 44-W-2 to die during training. An Army Air Forces report said the accident was caused by sparks from the plane's exhaust, which set fire to the fabric-covered tail and stabilizer. Betty was a good pilot. She did everything she had been trained to do. Betty Stine's death hung heavy over 44-W-2 as they hurried to complete their training before graduation.

EIGHT

Silver Wings and Santiago Blue

You'll go forth from here with your silver wings
Santiago blue and a heart that sings—
'Cause you ain't gonna be here no longer.

—WASP SONG

In March 1944, Marie Michell and 44-W-2 were too busy getting in the last of their 210 flying hours to pay much attention to the war news. U.S. firepower pounded Japanese-occupied territories in the Pacific, and an American flag was raised for the first time on Kwajalein Atoll in the Marshall Islands. In Europe, B-17s and B-24s bombed German targets. The casualty rate climbed during the fierce fighting in Anzio, Italy. Not only were soldiers killed there, but five American Army nurses died when their hospital took a direct hit from enemy airplanes.

When 44-W-2 returned from cross-country training, they found that their new dress uniforms had arrived. And what beautiful outfits they were! Jacket, skirt, and matching beret were made of fine, dark blue wool, white shirts, black four-in-hand ties, white gloves, black shoes, and hose completed the outfit. The wear and care of these uniforms had to conform to the military regulations of that time.

None of the trainees knew what Jackie Cochran had gone through to get these new uniforms. The first class of WASPs, 43-W-1, had put together their own uniforms of white blouses, khaki slacks, and matching caps. At their graduation, General Arnold noticed this as he gave the WASPs their wings, and he suggested to Jackie that the women needed new uniforms. This was just what she wanted to hear. The director was long aware of the importance of uniforms—how they distinguish the wearer and foster a sense of identity.

She worked for a year getting exactly what she wanted. When she asked to see the material for the uniforms, the quartermaster in charge of supplies directed her to a government warehouse, where there were piles of fabric used in WACs' uniforms. She wanted none of the pinkish-brown material. She paid her own money to have a uniform designed by an exclusive department store in New York City. She selected a dark blue—Santiago blue, she called it—fine wool cloth. Then she had two uniforms made: one in the pinkish-tan material, and the other in her blue. She chose two women as models and ushered both into General Arnold's office. On the spot, he would not decide between the uniforms, so she sought and got an audience with Gen. George Marshall, Army Chief of Staff. He selected the Santiago blue and guaranteed payment for the uniforms—about $175 for the jacket, skirt, and beret. Trainees had to spend about $100 for their shirts, shoes, ties, and undergarments. This was a financial hardship for some, but each woman gladly paid to have a complete outfit for graduation.

Graduation day was set for March 11. Jackie Cochran arrived on March 8 and spent most of her time conferring with Mrs. Deaton about graduation arrangements and other administrative matters. Miss Cochran had missed the previous three graduations, and word had it that the WASP director was pulling out all the stops for this ceremony. Rumors flew that high-ranking officials were coming. They proved to be true. On the 11th, seven Army Air Forces generals landed at Avenger Field. The most anticipated of all was the commencement speaker, Henry H. "Hap" Arnold, Commanding General of the United States Army Air Forces.

Long before he became a four-star general, Hap (so called because of his perpetual smile) Arnold was a legend among pilots. His career in aviation had begun literally with Wilbur and Orville Wright. Hap Arnold graduated from the U.S. Military Academy at West Point in 1907, and after a stint in the infantry, joined the Army Signal Corps. In 1909, the Signal Corps bought an airplane from the Wright brothers. Officials wanted to see if this new-fangled air machine might be used for more than delivering messages. The Signal Corps formed an aviation division and asked Arnold if he was interested in joining.

In 1911, Arnold and another young officer went to Dayton, Ohio where Wilbur and Orville Wright manufactured their planes. Under the tutelage of the Wright brothers, Arnold learned about the principles of flight and how planes were constructed. And he learned to fly the flimsy air machine himself. Hap Arnold later said, "More than anyone I have ever known or read about, the Wright brothers gave me the sense that nothing is impossible."[16]

Hap Arnold received his certification in 1911 as U. S. Army Aviator Number Two, one of only two fully trained pilots in the Aviation Service. He set out to show what the air machines could do and wound up spending most of his life trying to convince his military superiors of the need for these air machines. He became convinced that with guns mounted in planes, wars could be fought in the air. Arnold lobbied hard for the research and development of bombers and fighter planes. He also pushed for more training and more facilities in which to instruct the pilots.

When Pearl Harbor was bombed on December 7, 1941, the United States was woefully short of planes. The Army Air Corps (the name was changed to Army Air Forces in June 1942) had only 1,100 combat planes when it joined this global war. The need for planes and pilots became acute, even desperate.

Hap Arnold turned his extraordinary energy into obtaining them. He ordered plane development, harangued manufacturers, built air fields and training schools, and pleaded for more money from Congress. Throughout this chaotic time, Arnold had the support of President Roosevelt, Secretary of War Henry Stimson, and the brilliant architect of the war, Gen. George Marshall, Chief of Staff.

General Arnold never stopped pushing for a separate air force nor did he stop pushing those in authority. He openly criticized his superiors and came close to being court-martialed several times during his career, but the United States air force had come far under General Arnold's command. How important he was in developing military aviation is reflected in the statistics: In 1938 when Arnold was appointed chief of the Air Corps, there were only 20,000 men and a few hundred less-than-ready planes. By 1944 the Army Air Force had 2.4 million men and 80,000 aircraft. So when this legendary general stepped from his plane at Avenger Field, Marie Michell and her classmates could not have been more thrilled than if President Roosevelt himself had arrived.

The graduation ceremony was scheduled for 4:30 P.M. Marie and the rest of 44-W-2 lined up and marched into the gym to the martial music of the Big Spring Bombardier Band. Other Avenger classes marched in review.

Watching the proceedings on stage were Jackie Cochran and Ethel Sheehy, her second-in-command; Mrs. Deaton; the Avenger military officers; and the seven generals bedecked in their ribbons, medals, and stars. And there was Nancy Harkness Love, Executive WASP with the Ferrying Division.

Most of 44-W-2 saw Nancy Love for the first time on stage. This tall woman with striking blue eyes and steel-gray hair held many firsts in aviation. Born to a prominent midwestern family, she became hooked on flying after riding with a barnstormer. A few months later, at the age of sixteen, Nancy got her private pilot's license; two years later, she qualified for a commercial pilot's license. She dropped out of Vassar College to pursue flying full time.

When the war started in Europe in 1939, Nancy and her husband won a U. S. government contract to deliver American planes to Canada. Along with 32 male pilots, Nancy picked up planes from the manufacturers and flew them to the Canadian border. She taxied the aircraft to the boundary line, cut off the switch, and got out. The Canadian pilots then pushed and pulled the planes across the border and flew them to England and France. Nancy Love was the first woman to ferry planes in the United States.

Like Jackie Cochran, Nancy thought if the United States entered the war, women pilots could aid their country. In 1940, she wrote a plan for recruiting a small, select group of women pilots and sent it to Gen. Robert Olds, then head of the Ferry Command. He passed the idea along to Gen. Hap Arnold who turned down the plan, just as he would do later with Jackie Cochran's proposal.

That changed with the Japanese attack on Pearl Harbor. After war was declared, Nancy Love's husband took a position as deputy chief in the Air Transport Command. His boss, Gen. Harold Tunner, complained that he was short of pilots to deliver planes from the manufacturers to military bases. Robert Love suggested that General Tunner talk to Nancy. The general did so and was impressed. He asked her to submit a plan for recruiting and using women pilots.

Nancy Harkness Love, director of the Women's Auxiliary Ferry Squadron, leans against a PT-19 trainer. She tested nearly every type of plane produced for the Army Air Forces during World War II. *Courtesy of The Woman's Collection, Texas Woman's University*

Nancy's proposal went up the chain of command until it landed once more in General Arnold's office. Under circumstances not quite clear, the plan was approved. On September 10, 1942, Secretary of War Henry Stimson announced the formation of the Women's Auxiliary Ferry Squadron (WAFS) with Nancy Love as head. She was only 28 years old.

Nancy Love and Jackie Cochran were contrasts in personality and style. Nancy did not make waves as Jackie did, but she stood her ground when pushed. Unlike Jackie, Nancy was reserved and did not like publicity. She preferred flying to administrative duties, and before World War II was over, she would fly most of the planes made at the time—over seventy different types of aircraft. Those who worked with Nancy Love, including the military brass and the WASPs, admired and respected her.

In his graduation speech, General Arnold paid tribute to Nancy Love and Jackie Cochran for their vision and hard work. He said:

> I am looking forward to the day when Women's Airforce Service Pilots take the place of practically all AAF pilots in the U.S. for the duration of the war.
>
> The WASPs are doing an effective job of delivering aircraft in the U.S. from the smallest planes to big fighters, bombers, and transports. They fill the need for professional non-combat service in the country and Canada. For example, the Training Command uses many women pilots to ferry airplanes to and from certain bases for major repair or overhaul.
>
> However, in recent months the WASPs have assumed additional duties—towing targets in gunnery schools, acting as copilots on night searchlight missions and the like. Women pilots also are flying some of the weather planes which take meteorologists aloft. Indeed, this organization

has come to serve a variety of useful purposes in the Army
Air Force[s] organization. We can use and probably will continue to use as many WASPs as we can turn out for these
non-combat duties.

We are proud of you and welcome you as part of the
Army Air Force[s].[17]

After his speech, General Arnold handed out awards to some
members of 44-W-2 for their leadership abilities. He also presented the Air Medal to Barbara Erickson, the first WASP to be so
honored. She was one of the original WAFS, who was a flight
instructor when she was recruited by Nancy Love. Miss Erickson
presently served as WASP squadron commander of the 6th
Ferrying Group at Long Beach, California. First bestowed on
Amelia Earhart, the Air Medal was a special civilian award for
"meritorious service." During a five-day period in August 1943,
Barbara Erickson had made four, 2,000-mile deliveries, flying
three different types of aircraft.

And now for the moment Marie and 44-W-2 had spent six
grueling months for: the awarding of diplomas and the pinning
of wings. The silver-winged pins had diamond-shaped centers,
said to represent the shield of Athena, goddess of war. Jackie
Cochran's husband had paid for the wings of the first seven grad-
uating classes; the military bought the wings of the remaining
classes.

As Mrs. Deaton rose to call each graduate, she dropped the
list of names. When she picked up the papers, the names were
not in the same order in which the women had lined up. She
called Leona Golbinec's name first. It was a great honor to be
pinned first by General Arnold. The pinning of wings was usually
ceremonial, with the first set of wings actually being pinned and
the other wings being handed to the remaining women. The next
WASP in line was Kate Lee Harris. After General Arnold had

Lorraine Zillner, 44-W-2, receives her aviator's wings from Gen. Henry H. "Hap" Arnold at graduation on March 11, 1944. WASP wings, with a diamond-shaped center, were slightly smaller than standard pilot wings. *Courtesy of Lorraine Zillner Rodgers*

pinned Leona, Kate spoke up in her soft North Carolina accent and said, "Well, don't stop naow." [18]

He kept on going. After several pinnings, Jackie Cochran broke in, "Never mind, General, you don't have to do that."

General Arnold replied, "Never mind, Jackie, I enjoy doing this."[19]

And he pinned all forty-nine graduates. It was one of the greatest moments that Marie and her classmates ever experienced.

Jackie Cochran and Gen. Barton Yount then handed out the diplomas. The graduation ceremony ended with the singing of "The Star Spangled Banner," and everyone moved outside to the flight line for final review. But before adjourning, the classes sang to each other. In this Avenger tradition, the graduates sang first to the remaining classes, who responded in kind. Glancing sideways at each other and smiling, 44-W-2 broke into a spirited rendition of the infamous and forbidden, "Rugged But Right."

> I just called up to tell you that I'm rugged but right!
> A rambling woman, a gambling woman, drunk every night.
> A porterhouse steak three times a day for my board,
> That's more than any decent gal in town can afford!
> I've got a big electric fan to keep me cool while I eat,
> A tall and handsome man to keep me warm while I sleep!
> I'm a rambling woman, a gambling woman and BOY am I
>   tight!
> I just called up to tell you that I'm rugged but right!
> HO-HO-HO—Rugged but right![20]

Jackie Cochran sat silent and stone-faced, and Gen. H. H. "Hap" Arnold roared.

NINE

Careful Where You Aim, Sir

*It makes no difference what a pilot's reproductive organs are
shaped like. It's skill that matters.*

—GEN. CHUCK YEAGER

By spring of 1944, the nature of the war had changed in favor of
the Allies. Aerial bombing reduced German cities to rubble;
munitions, factories, and transportation systems were laid to
waste. The class of 44-W-2 read this news about the overseas military campaigns, and although their service was limited to within
the continental United States, they were eager to do their part for
the war effort.

After graduation, the women packed their belongings and
left for ten days leave at home. Shortly before she graduated,
each pilot had a chance to indicate what planes she wished to fly
during her service, where she wanted to be based (no closer than
150 miles to home), and friends with whom she wished to serve.

Mrs. Deaton looked at these preferences in light of the
women's flight training records and evaluations. She devised rating sheets similar to those used for male cadets. The flight and

ground school instructors as well as the physical trainer submitted their ratings; the class staff adviser and class student officers also gave their evaluations. Mrs. Deaton listed the demerits for each student. She then compiled a chart and each graduate was given an overall rating.

Jackie Cochran sent the military's requests for the new women pilots to Mrs. Deaton. Matching the women's preferences and rankings with the base requests made for a giant juggling act. Sometimes the women's wishes had to be ignored because of other considerations. For example, the tallest and strongest women were chosen to fly B-17s because these requirements were necessary for piloting the huge four-engine bombers. Another example was when there was a special assignment. Such a request came from the base commander at Dodge City, Kansas. Twenty members of 44-W-2 were assigned here for transitional training on the B-26 bomber.

The other 44-W-2 graduates were scattered over the country. Fifteen were assigned to the ferrying divisions; five, including Marie Michell, went to the Fifth Ferry Group at Love Field (not named for Nancy Love), Dallas, Texas; five were sent to the Sixth Ferry Group in Long Beach, California; and five served in the Second Ferry Group at New Castle Army Air Base in Wilmington, Delaware. The rest of the class was assigned singly or in pairs to other bases.

From this point on, the women pilots were in the military system and were subject to transfer, just as male military pilots were. Most of 44-W-2, including Marie, would be transferred later to other bases. Although they were Civil Service employees, the WASPs were proud to be in the military, serving where they were needed. They would ask for no favors or exceptions to the rules. They knew they would do a good job, even though they had to work harder. They had the skills and confidence. They were tough enough.

On March 22, the twenty WASPs from 44-W-2 arrived at Dodge City Army Air Base, wearing their new dress uniforms. Located on the western plains of Kansas, it was a large base that trained pilots—American and Allied—to fly the medium-sized B-26, a twin-engine bomber. The women pilots of 44-W-2 had not been given training in flying twin-engine planes, but they were eager to learn.

The WASPs checked in and were assigned to their own quarters. The base quartermaster issued them their flying equipment: goggles, a leather flying helmet, an oxygen mask, a pilot's navigation kit, a leather pilot's jacket, flying gloves, sunglasses, hand-held transmitter/receiver, parachute and parachute bag, earphones, microphone, and a small suitcase called a B-4 bag. They were also given clothing, which included a waist-length wool Eisenhower jacket; a flight cap; flight coveralls; a trench raincoat; a parka-type overcoat; and a duffel bag. These articles were called government issue, or "G.I." for short, and had to be returned when the women left the base permanently.

Finally, the WASPs got their closeup look at the B-26 *Marauder.* The plane was sleek and shiny and looked like a flying torpedo, which was one of its many names. It had a short wingspan, which gave rise to another nickname, the "Flying Prostitute"—because it had no visible means of support. This bomber had a bad reputation among the military pilots. It was also called the "Murderer," the "Widow Maker," and other frightening names. It was a "hot" or an unforgiving plane, one that did not allow pilots to make mistakes. Rumor had it that because the commander at Dodge City had a problem getting the men to fly the bomber, he requested WASPs to embarrass the men into doing it.

The initial B-26 model had two 1,850-horsepower engines, which pushed its speed to over 300 miles per hour (mph). It had a wing span of 65 ft. and could carry up to 5,800 lbs. of bombs.

Even as the WASPs were training at Dodge City, B-26s were drop-ping more than a thousand tons of bombs on German-occupied France and Belgium. In spite of its scary reputation at home, the B-26 had the lowest loss rate of any bomber during combat.

Some of 44-W-2 had asked to be assigned to Dodge City, even though they had heard the bad rumors about the B-26. Esther Noffke was one. From the moment she had seen a B-26 come in at Sweetwater, she knew that she wanted to fly this plane. Esther was half an inch short of the 5'6" requirement, so she put down the B-26 three times in the spaces listing plane choices. Fran Smith was shorter, but Mrs. Deaton made an exception for her because she was such a good pilot during training. Madeline Sullivan was another who wanted the plane because of its high horsepower rating.

The WASPs had to complete seventy-five flying hours during the B-26 transitional training. They found the plane was hard to handle and training was tough. To take off, the pilot had to raise the nosewheel off the ground by pulling back on the yoke with her left hand while keeping her right hand on the throttle. It was tempting to use both hands on the yoke, so the instructor would promptly whack the pilot's right hand if she removed it from the throttle. One of Madeline Sullivan's friends, a boxer, showed the women how to do various exercises to increase hand and arm strength. They also constantly worked squeeze balls with their left hands.

WASPs learned that to master the *Marauder* they had to adjust to the instability of the plane and be constantly attentive. Landing this aircraft was especially tricky. The pilot had to bring it in at no less than 135 mph. If the plane came in slower, it would stall and crash. And unlike other planes where the approach is gradual, the B-26 came in at a dive, flattened out, and landed like a brick.

In addition to their B-26 flight training, the WASPs attended ground school. Female pilots took the same courses and sat in the same classes as the male lieutenants. The WASPs' aptitude surprised many men at the base, who thought women did not have the ability to master complex aircraft systems, an attitude typical at that time. In the most important course that covered B-26 procedures, they earned higher scores than the men on the tests covering hydraulic and electrical systems, and they also did better on overall mechanical operation. The instructor complimented the WASPs on their superior performances, noting that the male members of the class could have benefitted from more serious study of the course textbook.

Of the twenty WASPs at Dodge City, one left for personal reasons and six either washed out or felt they were not suited for the B-26. They were reassigned to other bases, where they towed targets from smaller planes or tested repaired aircraft. The graduates of B-26 training were sent to Gowen Army Air Base in Boise, Idaho where they would tow targets for gunnery practice. Gowen was the final training base for aerial gunners before they were sent into combat. Gunners practiced shooting at a moving object called a tow target. It was a rectangular canvas sleeve, about twenty feet long that was connected by a heavy steel cable to the back of the tow plane. When released by the engineer, the target floated about 1,500 feet behind the tow plane.

The gunners trained for accuracy in two ways: with cameras and with live ammunition. Camera practice used cameras mounted on the guns. As the tow target passed, the gunners aimed and shot at the target while the cameras recorded the action. Each gunner's film was then developed and analyzed to see how accurate he was.

Towing targets from the temperamental B-26 was far more hazardous, even for simulated gunnery practice. A B-24 bomber carried the gunners. For gunnery practice, the B-24s flew in formation with a certain distance between each plane. The WASP pilot with a

While a WASP pilot flew the A-24 *Dauntless* dive bomber, a tow-reel operator in the rear seat handled the tow target that the male trainees shot at. This A-24 was used to train ground artillery gunners. *Courtesy of The Woman's Collection, Texas Woman's University*

tow target flew above them and then dived down through the formation while gunners "shot" at the target with cameras. The WASP pilot had to monitor her dive and pull out at the right moment or the B-26 would sink. And she could not get too close to the B-24s because of the danger of hitting one of the planes.

Such an incident happened to Joan Whelan and Fran Smith. As the first pilot, Fran took the plane up. Joan took over the controls once they were in the air. As Joan dived into the formation, one of the B-24 pilots urged her to come in closer. She took the dare. When the tow target was released, it jolted the plane and Joan hit the tail of the B-24. The B-24 lost part of its tail section;

the B-26 had a hole in the right wing. Fran took over the controls again and both planes managed to land safely, due to skill and luck. Most midair collisions are fatal.

Most of the gunnery practice at Gowen used live ammunition. Those WASPs who flew the B-26 for live gunnery practice had one of the most dangerous assignments that any pilot could have. At first, WASPs did not worry much about the live ammunition until they heard about a pilot at another base who had his foot shot off because the gunners mistook the tow plane for the target. One gunner hit the nose of the B-26 that Madeline Sullivan and Sadie Hawkins were flying. Another time, the two had an engine shot out and had to make an emergency landing.

During live ammunition practice, the command pilot made a straight pass on one side of the B-24 formation while gunners shot at the target. Then the B-26 pilot radioed to the other planes to cease firing, crossed over in front of the B-24 formation, and passed on the other side, making a rectangular pattern. When target practice was over, the B-26 pilot dropped off the tow target at an auxiliary field where officials picked it up and evaluated the gunners' accuracy.

Some of the scariest moments happened while just flying the B-26. Fran Smith had a close call when an engine quit in midair. The B-26 was a difficult enough plane to land with both engines, but to set the plane down with only one engine was extremely risky. Fran had to control the propeller blades of the disabled engine to keep them from whirling uncontrollably, causing excessive vibration and drag. From a control button in the cockpit, she turned the blades to a 90° angle. The edge of the blades then faced toward the line of flight. This procedure was called "feathering the prop." With the blades secured, Fran came in and set the plane down in a perfect landing.

Marge Gilbert and Pat Patterson also had engine failure in their B-26 when the drive shaft in one engine broke. The two pilots had to get the plane down from 10,000 feet. They feathered the prop and radioed into the control tower. Because it was an emergency, the tower cleared them for number one landing.

Word flew throughout the base that two WASPs in the air were in trouble. Everyone ran to watch the plane. Not only was an engine out on the crippled B-26, but the hydraulic system was not working either, which meant the landing wheels would not come down. The engineer on board finally worked the wheels loose, but the plane was over the runway by this time. The two pilots had to try to land on an adjacent runway, which was crowded with parked planes.

As she came in, Marge held the plane straight and aimed between the rows of planes. She set the B-26 down without blowing a tire or hitting another plane. A huge cheer went up from the crowd. Marge sat in the plane, her knees shaking so much that she could not walk. The men at the base had been skeptical about the women pilots, but with Marge Gilbert's feat, the WASPs were considered "in" at Gowen.

But if there were hair-raising experiences on the B-26, there were also unexpected moments of beauty. Mary Ellen Keil and Ruth Woods experienced such a moment. They had to fly Gowen base officers to Salt Lake City, Utah for business and the officers did not finish until dark.

Even though WASPs were trained in night flying, they were not supposed to fly B-26s at night. Still everyone had to get back to the base in Idaho.

The two lifted off with 4,000 lbs. of horsepower propelling them through the sky. Snow covered the ground and it was a clear night. They flew over the white, still landscape with the feel of the plane's power in their bones. An overwhelming sense of awe and peace enveloped them.

Every pilot lives for such moments.

TEN

You Call This Plane Fixed?

Flying is the second greatest experience in the world.
Landing is the first.

—UNKNOWN

Twelve members of 44-W-2 had assignments flight testing repaired planes at various training bases. The Army Air Forces listed these jobs as "engineering or mechanical testing" and those who tested the planes as "engineering test pilots." While these test pilots did not have to master planes as challenging as the B-26, their work could still be hazardous.

After the plane was repaired, the WASP took it up and flew it through certain routine maneuvers. If the plane performed satisfactorily, she brought the plane in and checked it off with the mechanic. The WASPs developed good working relationships with the maintenance personnel. Their lives depended on their mechanics.

The WASP pilots also did another kind of test flying called "slow-timing." After 100 flying hours, each plane was pulled from flight training. Mechanics took the engine out and gave it a thor-

ough check. Worn or stressed engine parts were replaced; sometimes a plane received a completely new engine. For testing after
the 100-hour check, the pilot would take the plane up at the slow-
est possible speed, then fly it for slow-paced maneuvers. After
twenty or thirty minutes of slow-timing, the pilot "opened 'er up"
at full throttle, and she flew the plane hard—in much the same
way an inexperienced trainee might.

At Napier Army Air Base in Alabama, Kate Lee Harris and
Leona Golbinec tested AT-6s. One day, Kate Lee had an incident
that had an unintended, happy ending. She was out flying when
she saw a storm approaching. She radioed the control tower to
see if planes had been grounded. The man in the control tower
said in a demeaning tone, "Why would we call off flying?"[21]

The storm grew more ominous and Kate Lee decided to land
anyway. As she came in, a terrible dust storm hit and the high
winds tipped her plane on its nose. She did not know that all flying had been called off. She feared that other pilots would not
see her and would land on top of her. She sat there looking like
a clown with two white spots around her eyes where her goggles
had been; the rest of her face was covered with dust.

When the wind died down and the dust cleared, a Jeep drove
up, and—as Kate described him—"a little shavetail Officer of the
Day" stepped out. Kate was so angry and scared that she exploded
at the man. The officer, Bob Adams, would later become her husband.

Leona and Kate Lee also ferried planes and personnel to
other bases and taught instrument flying if needed. Unlike other
class members who were moved around to different bases, Leona
and Kate Lee spent all their service at Napier because the base
commander did not want them to leave. When the WASP program was disbanded, the base commander gave all the WASPs an
opportunity to return as Link trainers and instrument instructors. Most did.

Ruth Petry and Mary Strok went to Courtland Army Air Field in Alabama, where the two did maintenance testing on BT-13s and BT-15s. Prior to their arrival, testing was done by flight instructors who were only too glad to have women take over these duties because it freed the men to do other tasks.

The male cadets in training at Courtland were surprised to find out that most of the women were skilled pilots before becoming WASPs. They were even more impressed when they learned how many flying hours the women had before they entered Avenger Field. (Ruth had 270 hours.) Most male cadets at Courtland had no flying experience prior to their military training.

Doris Elkington Hamaker reported for duty at Stockton Army Air Base after graduation. She was the first WASP at the advanced training base, where she was put up in the nurses' quarters. Doris had been at the base for a few weeks, testing AT-17 advanced trainers, when one day, she was told to report to the operations officer. With much trepidation, she walked into his office. There she saw her best friend, Gini Dulaney, sitting on the corner of the officer's desk, swinging her leg. Doris took her to meet the commander and Gini asked if he had a place for her at his base. The next week she was transferred from Merced Army Air Field to Stockton.

The two WASPs, along with three men, tested AT-17s as the planes came off the maintenance line. They flew together as pilot and copilot in the two-seater plane. One tested one thing while the other tested something else; the work was faster that way.

One day the maintenance officer at the base, a major, wanted to go up with the WASPs when they tested a UC-78. He was grounded because he had broken his back in an aircraft accident. None of the military pilots allowed him to fly with them because they would have been court-martialed. The major begged the two women to take him. They finally relented and sneaked him on the plane. He sat in the back, while Gini and Doris sat in the pilots' seats. After takeoff, the plane's flaps stuck in a fixed position. They all knew if this was not corrected the plane would continue to float in the air. The major said, "Oh, my God."

"Relax, Major," Gini said, "This happens to us all the time. No big sweat."

Then an engine went out. The pilots were over a heavily congested area so they could not abandon the plane, and they could not bail out because the major had no parachute. Gini called the Stockton control tower for an emergency landing. The controller cleared the field and directed the women to make a straight-in landing. He also called the commanding officer, the officer of the day, an ambulance, and fire trucks. He ordered complete air silence. It was dead quiet. Then over the intercom came a voice from another plane. The voice said, "A woman's place is in the home."[22]

Gini and Doris were far too occupied to take offense at this remark, but they laughed about it later. Meanwhile, the major wanted to land the plane. He moved to the first pilot's seat and made a perfect landing. During the confusion on the ground, he hopped out of the plane without being seen. For weeks, everyone complimented Gini on her perfect landing, and she could not tell them the truth.

Doris and Gini had another incident in a UC-78. They had to test the plane after an oil line had been repaired. They took off and suddenly were engulfed in a huge, black cloud of smoke. They realized that the mechanic had failed to fix the oil line.

A voice from the intercom yelled that the plane was on fire. Gini replied calmly that she saw the smoke. The WASPs circled and landed. The crew chief ran over, his face white. "What happened?" he asked.

Gini said, "I'll tell you what happened. You didn't fix the damned oil line."

"I did," he said.

Gini was furious. She scooped up a handful of oil that covered the wing and smeared the oil across the mechanic's face.

"What's that?"[23] she asked.

The WASPs were upset by the mechanic's carelessness. Not only because their lives were placed in jeopardy, but also because a male trainee—a future combat pilot—might have been killed in the plane. Doris and Gini had a rewarding stay at Stockton. When the commander's family came to live at the base, he asked the women to take his daughter around and introduce her. They took his request to be a great compliment.

During their assignments, all the WASPs tried to follow the bill in Congress that would give them military status. From the beginning of the WASP program, it was anticipated that the women pilots would be made part of the military as were the women in the Army (WACs), the Navy (WAVEs), the Coast Guard (SPARs), and the Women Marines. Gen. Hap Arnold and Director Jackie Cochran had agreed to the WASPs' initial civilian status in 1942 because pilots were desperately needed and there was not enough time to go through Congress for military status and funding. Now, with their proven work record, it was time to make these women pilots a part of the Army Air Forces.

In February 1944, Representative John Costello of California submitted his proposal, bill H.R. 4219, to the Military Affairs Committee. The bill would confer Army Air Forces commissions on all women pilots in duty. If passed, the WASPs would be entitled to the same insurance, hospitalization, and death benefits granted to male officers.

During that same month, the Army Air Forces had shut down the War Training Service and the civilian flight training program. This meant that some 14,000 civilian male pilots and male cadets would face active military duty. If they wanted to be military

WASPs Eloise Huffhines (44-W-4), Mildred Davidson (44-W-4), Kit MacKethan
(44-W-2), and Clara Jo Marsh (44-W-3), sporting their Santiago blue uniforms, walk
in front of a B-24 *Liberator* at Maxwell Field in Alabama. More than 18,000 B-24s
were built during World War II. *Courtesy of The Woman's Collection, Texas Woman's
University*

pilots, they would have to meet the same stringent requirements
and go through the same Army Air Forces training program, as
the WASPs did. If not, then they would join ground crews or be
drafted into the infantry. Few civilian pilots wanted to be foot soldiers. They complained to their congressmen and to the press,
charging that the women pilots were taking their jobs. Editorial
writers and columnists called the WASP program a "racket," a
"blunder," and "Jackie's Glamour Girls."

The Military Affairs Committee scheduled a hearing on bill
H.R. 4219 on March 22, about the time 44-W-2 reported for duty
to their bases. General Arnold testified before the committee,
arguing that the Women Airforce Service Pilots were a necessary
part of the war effort, and that they deserved the same benefits as

the men under his command currently had. The WASPs, he said, had met the highest standards of the Army Air Forces.

Later, in closed session, General Arnold told the committee that male pilots had been reluctant to tow targets and test repaired planes; the women pilots willingly did this drudgery work. They had also climbed into the B-26, the Widow Maker, the same plane some of his officers were leery of flying. The general praised the WASPs' attitudes. He said that they were grateful, dutiful, and loyal—attributes that the military prized. The Military Affairs Committee recommended bill H.R. 4219, and it went to the House Rules Committee, which determined the bills that would go to the full House of Representatives.

With the support of the secretary of war and the Roosevelt administration, bill H.R. 4219 was considered by the House Rules Committee. Here, the issue of funding for the WASP training program was raised. The money for the program had come from the general military budget. Congressmen complained they had not voted funds for training women pilots. Not only were the WASPs accused of taking the men's jobs, but the program was criticized for siphoning money that should have gone elsewhere in the military.

The House Rules Committee recommended that the bill be sent to the House for a vote. However, they attached two riders: the women's pilot training program should be discontinued; and the male civilian pilots would be granted military status—if they met the Army Air Forces standards.

Bill H.R. 4219 came to the House for a final vote on June 19, 1944. The debate lasted 42 hours. On June 21st, the vote was taken; 188 congressmen voted no, 169 voted yes, and 73 did not vote. The bill to militarize the WASPs failed. Never once during the debate was the WASPs' competency and performance questioned.

At Avenger Field, 44-W-10 had already started their training.

They were allowed to finish, but they would be the last class to graduate from the only women's pilot training program in U.S. history. The next class had received their orders to report for training on June 30. Deedie Deaton notified these women immediately, telling them not to report. However, some had already begun the long train trip to Sweetwater; the military paid their transportation back home.

The women pilots already in service would continue to work but without any military benefits. A few WASPs did not want to be militarized; they either had small children or didn't want to be locked into a military structure. But most of the WASPs, including Marie Michell, were bitterly disappointed. They wanted the benefits, but more than that, they wanted that official stamp of approval.

But the women pilots on duty still had work to complete. They had to finish their jobs of towing targets, testing planes, ferrying men and aircraft, instructing, and the other duties they were asked to do. But they would not forget—and many would not forgive—the fact that Congress had failed to give them military status.

ELEVEN

We Can Fly Anything in This Man's Army

No big deal. No mental genius. Just hard work.

—GEN. CHUCK YEAGER

During the first two years of World War II, the Army Air Forces desperately needed pilots to deliver planes. The Women Airforce Service Pilots helped to ferry planes from the manufacturers to training bases or to certain coastal cities where they were then flown or shipped overseas. Fifteen graduates of 44-W-2 asked for this important duty in March 1944.

Marie Michell was assigned to the Fifth Ferry Group at Love Field near Dallas. Like the other graduates, she had ten days leave before she reported for duty. She went home with her mother who had attended the Avenger ceremony; it was the first time Marie had seen her family in six months. When she reported to Love Field on March 22, she joined classmates Jean Hascall Cole, Shorty Stafford, Lorraine Zillner, and her best friend, Kit MacKethan.

Love Field was a large air base that dated back to World War I. Like all major ferry bases, it was located near one or more airplane manufacturers. It was about thirty miles from North American Aviation, which produced AT-6s, B-25 bombers, P-51s, the pursuit or fighter planes, and BT-9 and BT-14 basic trainers.

About 140 WASPs were stationed at Love Field at the time Marie and her classmates arrived. When they checked in, they took an oath of office, filled out forms, and had orientation with Delphine Bohn, their squadron commander. She looked after the WASPs' welfare, maintained discipline, acted as liaison with the flight operations office, and did the military paperwork relating to the WASPs. Miss Bohn reported to the base commander, to Nancy Love, who was her immediate superior, and to WASP Director Jackie Cochran.

The WASPs' basic pay was $250 a month (about $2,600 in today's money) or $3,000 a year ($31,200). In addition, they were given a travel allowance of $6.00 ($62.40) a day for expenses when they delivered planes. On base, the women pilots paid for their meals at the officers' mess and about $15 ($156) a month for their quarters. Hospital care cost $1.25 ($13) a day.

On base, the WASPs were housed in two, two-story barracks, where Marie and Kit shared a room. To get from their living quarters to the mess hall or flight line, the pilots took the "Fifth Ferry-Go-Round," an open air bus that operated around the clock. The bus seldom stopped, but moved slowly so that personnel hopped on and off as the vehicle circled the base.

Each WASP was issued flight clothing and equipment. Every ferry pilot was entitled to receive coveralls, a pilot's leather jacket, flying gloves, goggles, sunglasses, and a summer cloth flying helmet. For cold weather flying, they were issued leather, two-piece, fleece-lined flight suits and leather flying helmets.

Flying equipment included: a flight calculator, navigation plotter, handheld transmitter/receiver, headset, microphone, military watch, a B-4 bag to carry personal items, a briefcase, and plane seat cushions. In addition each pilot was given a parachute and a parachute bag with her name on it. When she returned to her home base, she had to turn in the parachute, which was inspected for tears. She picked it up when she was placed on flight orders again.

Ferry pilots who had to deliver planes with top secret equipment were issued .45-caliber pistols with ammunition. They were taught how to use the weapons and given target practice. The pistol was checked out when the pilot received her flight orders, and she had to return it when she came back to the base. There were no reports of any WASPs who had to use their pistols.

Every flier had a *Pilot's Information File* of regulations, procedures, flying safety, and up-to-date memoranda. She was issued a flight kit of forms, orders, and first aid supplies, such as sulpha powder to use for wounds and self-injected morphine for pain.

At Love Field, the WASPs reported at 8:00 A.M. to Delphine Bohn's office where they received their flight orders. If they had to deliver new planes, they hopped on the Ferry-Go-Round to catch the bus that went to North American Aviation.

When the ferry pilots arrived at the manufacturing plant, they saw the shiny new planes parked with their engines already running. Each pilot visually inspected her plane and checked Form One, the plane's logbook. Then she took the aircraft up and flew it slowly for about thirty minutes to break in the engine and to determine if the plane had any defects. If there were no problems during the test flight, she brought the plane back, marked "A-OK" on Form One, and signed for the plane. Before she left for her destination, she checked the weather reports and calculated her flight route on the map.

Flying a primary trainer at 105 mph, took a week or more for a pilot to deliver a plane from one coast to another. The faster basic trainer could be sped cross-country in two or three days, depending on weather conditions. A pilot who ferried one of these small planes had to make numerous refueling stops and

Virginia Williams Archer (43-W-5), in the B-17 *Flying Fortress* navigator's compart-
ment, plots her flight course from Columbus, Ohio to Houston, Texas. The ten-hour
route required careful planning before takeoff. *Courtesy of The Woman's Collection,
Texas Woman's University*

overnight stays along the way. If she flew with the sun, at the end of the day she stepped from her plane with one side of her face glowing scarlet and sporting one white goggle eye.

Every pilot was trained to constantly monitor a multitude of things. She would glance down to see the landmarks indicated on her map and look straight ahead to a fixed object or a point on the horizon to keep her bearings. She also kept an eye on the dials and gauges that indicated fuel, speed, altitude, direction, and other measurements. And always, she scanned the sky around and above her, watching for storms and other aircraft.

The pilot flying an open cockpit plane had a totally sensory experience. She heard the roar of the engine and felt the wind slice into exposed skin. Even during the summer, pilots wore their flight suits because it was cold at higher altitudes. The smell of oil and gasoline permeated the small plane. The pilot tasted the grit of the dust that flew up her nostrils and into her mouth. But most of all, she saw. She saw the bluest of blue in the sky, the whitest of white in the clouds, and all the colors in between. And she felt fortunate to be able to do what she loved best.

The Ferrying Division issued strict guidelines to fliers who delivered planes. Pilots had to land the aircraft an hour before sundown; night flying was not permitted. They could not fly during certain kinds of weather, such as snow and fog; if they ran into storms, they had to land at the nearest airport. Except for landing and takeoff, they could not fly below 1,500 feet. Every ferry pilot knew that the plane had to be delivered as quickly and as safely as possible.

A pilot of a primary trainer plane did not have a radio, so when she arrived at the base, she got in the traffic pattern and waited for a green light from the control tower. After she landed, she taxied to where she should park the plane. Taking her flight gear, including the parachute, she reported to the base operations office, completed her paperwork, and received a delivery receipt for the plane.

Sometimes, if it was a short trip and the pilot got in well before sundown, she might have to make a return trip that day to home base. Or she might have orders to deliver another plane. Ferry pilots generally had to fly from sunup to sundown; they were expected to make the most of their daylight flying hours.

Most of the time, the pilot remained overnight and had to find a place to sleep. At a military base, she could probably get a room in the nurses' or WACs' quarters, but if she landed at a local airport, she had to find a room in a hotel or boarding house. During the war, there were many people in transit, with military men on their way to bases or wives and families seeing off their husbands, fathers, and sons. The ferry pilot might have to spend the night in the hotel or train station lobby, using her parachute as a pillow.

The WASPs were expected to keep their uniforms looking clean and pressed at all times. But after spending several days sitting in a cockpit, their clothing got dirty and developed baggy knees and sagging seats. The women did the best they could under the circumstances: they brushed down and spot-cleaned their uniforms; some pilots had their own travel irons, while others pressed their slacks by placing them between a mattress and boxspring.

If the WASP had orders to pick up and deliver another plane the next day, she arose before dawn and reported to the base flight line an hour before sunup. She checked her plane carefully before she signed for it, even going so far as sticking a finger in the gas tank to make sure the plane had been fueled. She could not rely on the gauges or the mechanics to tell her everything was in working order. The aircraft was her responsibility.

After her final stop, the ferry pilot had to get back to home base by the fastest means possible so she could deliver another plane. If she were near a large city, she boarded a commercial plane. All ferry pilots had Priority II flying status on the nation's airlines. This meant that they could bump anyone off the plane, including politicians or movie stars—and they did. Only someone carrying direct orders from the president of the United States or emergency medical personnel had a higher flying priority than the ferry pilots.

Returning pilots could also hop a ride on a military cargo plane, jokingly called Airline SNAFU (Situation Normal, All Fouled Up) or TARFU (Things Are *Really* Fouled Up). They avoided taking cargo planes if they could. Onboard, they sat in aluminum bucket seats along the sides of the plane, with a large coffee can that served as the toilet; and there was no food or water. But worse, the plane might not take off unless it had a full load, or it might make several stops along the way. Sometimes it was faster and more comfortable to take the train.

If the WASP was really lucky, she might have an order to deliver a plane back to Dallas. Often she got back between meals, when the mess hall was closed. The American Red Cross operated a twenty-four-hour "survival station" run by women volunteers. At the station, the pilot could get hot soup, sandwiches, cookies, hot coffee, milk, and soft drinks. She then caught the Ferry-Go-Round to get back to her quarters. Sometimes, returning pilots and crews on the bus were so exhausted they fell asleep standing up, gripping the handrails.

If the WASP returned to base before 10:00 P.M., she had to report to Miss Bohn's office the next morning for another flight assignment. If she got in after ten, she had the next day off. Of course, she tried to work her flight schedule so that she arrived late, but days off were rare. Most of the ferry pilots flew a grueling schedule of seven days a week. When one WASP begged for a Sunday off, Delphine Bohn was heard replying, "When the fellows are in the trenches they don't have Saturday and Sunday off. What do you think this is?"[24]

One of the most dangerous jobs any ferry pilot had to fly was delivering old planes to be "mothballed" or scrapped. When a plane could no longer be repaired, the mechanics put a red X on the plane's Form One, which indicated the plane was not safe to fly. Yet this aircraft had to be moved, and some WASPs got the jobs of flying these planes. Often they had tires that blew on landing, engines that failed, or had pieces of the plane fall off during flight.

All the ferry pilots came back from deliveries with stories. Kit MacKethan had a favorite. Once while ferrying a plane to the West Coast, she stopped in El Paso for the night. She had time to go over the border into Juarez, Mexico. While walking down the street, she saw a man selling Chihuahuas for $10 apiece. She bought one of the little dogs and put him in her B-4 bag with his head sticking out. The Chihuahua flew with her until she had a chance to give him to her mother when she made a delivery in North Carolina.

At the Sixth Ferry Group in Long Beach Army Air Base in California, five members of 44-W-2—Anne Berry, Margaret Ehlers, Muriel Lindstrom, Mary McCrea, and Alice Montgomery—ferried trainer planes and multi-engine aircraft. They flew mostly as copilots on the B-17 and B-24 bombers and the C-47 cargo planes.

The C-47 was one of the most significant planes of World War II. Officially named the *Skytrain*, everyone called it the "Gooney Bird," after the ungainly albatross of the Pacific. This cargo plane, made by the Douglas Aircraft Company, had twin engines that provided 2,400 lbs. of horsepower, had a wingspan of 95', and flew a top speed of 229 mph. It had double doors and reinforced floors to carry heavy loads and could be converted to a medical facility in a matter of hours. The *Skytrain* carried medics, flight nurses, and up to twenty-four wounded with their litters securely fastened to the inside walls of the plane's fuselage, or body. It could also function as a surgical unit and dispensary.

The C-47 played an important role in the D-Day invasion, the great Allied assault against Germany and Italy on June 6, 1944. As infantrymen landed on the beaches of France, C-47s dropped airborne troops and gliders behind German lines. But the transport plane was most famous for flying over the Himalayas, or as the pilots called this mountain range, the "Hump." The cargo planes were used by the Allies to carry supplies to the Chinese army. Taking off from British bases in India, pilots flew up to 19,000 feet over mountain passes in some of the most brutal weather conditions on earth. If a plane went down, those on board almost always died, although a few miraculously managed to walk out of the mountains. The WASPs who copiloted these behemoths knew of the bravery of the Hump pilots, and they felt a particular pride in ferrying these important war planes.

Five ferry pilots of 44-W-2 went to the Second Ferry Group, headquartered at New Castle Army Air Base in Wilmington, Delaware. Phyllis Tobias's assignment was to pick up PT-19s from Hagerstown, Pennsylvania and deliver them to Chickasaw, Oklahoma, a three-day journey. As Phyllis flew over the Blue Ridge Mountains, she thought they were the biggest mountains she had ever seen. This was wonderful, she thought.

Her response at viewing an unseen part of the country was not unusual. Long-distance travel, whether by automobile, train, or plane, was an uncommon experience during those days. Most ferry pilots had flown only in their local areas, so when they delivered planes, they saw the physical beauty of the continental United States for the first time.

Flying in the East, they looked down upon the forested mountains of the Catskills and saw the mists on the Great Smoky Mountains; they flew over the verdant valleys of West Virginia and Kentucky. Heading west, they crossed the broad Mississippi, snaking its way southward, and they saw the iron ore barges on the Great Lakes. They looked down on the patchwork squares of green corn in Iowa and the golden fields of wheat stretching as far as the eye could see on the Great Plains. They soared over the snow-covered Rockies, the Sierra, and the Cascades. In the Southwest they flew directly toward the burning sun, and when they came out of the operations office at sunset, they saw the same sky streaked with orange and red and then finally fade to purple.

Then the ferry pilots understood why Katherine Lee Bates penned the words to "America the Beautiful." And they knew what the men overseas were fighting for, and why they—the WASPs—flew.

TWELVE

Other Planes, Other Places

The suspense, never knowing what the next day would bring. The excitement. Excitement. That's the best word in the dictionary.

—DOROTHY KOCHER OLSON, WASP 43-W-4

Jackie Cochran experimented constantly with the WASP program. From the initial goal of ferrying aircraft, she had expanded the women's duties to include towing targets and testing planes. Cochran had put her pilots in the biggest military planes to prove that women were capable of handling the giant aircraft, and she jumped at the chance to put her WASPs into dangerous B-26s because she thought they could do it. Cochran also had another project for her women pilots.

During the spring and summer of 1944, she sent WASPs in small groups of fifty each to the Army Air Forces Strategic Command School in Orlando, Florida. This prestigious school gave advanced training to American and Allied military officers. When she first thought of this, she anticipated that the WASPs would eventually be commissioned as military officers. Even after the defeat of the Costello bill in June, Jackie wanted her pilots to continue with advanced training. Marie Michell and Kit MacKethan were among the members of 44-W-2 who participated in this program.

The month-long training was intensive. For six days a week, eight hours every day, the WASPs attended classes in military law, principles of leadership, military customs, intelligence operations, and survival skills. They also took advanced meteorology and navigation, physical training, and drill. They spent their remaining time on field trips in which they viewed air battle films, saw how the radar system (developed successfully in the late 1930s) worked, and learned about weapons.

One of the most interesting things about the Orlando school was its international milieu. The WASPs met officers from Great Britain, France, Turkey, and the Soviet Union. Among them were Soviet women pilots who flew dangerous bombing missions for their country. One of these combat pilots had shot down seventeen German aircraft! Male officers and WASPs were awed by the bravery and valor of these Soviet women pilots.

In August 1944, most members of 44-W-2 received orders transferring them to other bases. Because fewer combat missions were being flown in Europe, many male pilots were being released from fighter duties and moved into jobs such as towing targets. Fewer pilots were now being trained for the war so there was less need for ferrying trainer planes. The reassignments of 44-W-2 reflected these realities.

The B-26 tow target pilots at Gowen Army Air Base in Idaho were transferred to different bases, flying various aircraft. Four were moved to Dyersburg, Tennessee where they towed targets from the liaison L-5s and L-6s, the smallest of the powered military aircraft. These planes were also called "puddle jumpers" or "grasshoppers" because of their ability to get in and out of places with no runways. The liaison's small size was suited for scouting and observation purposes. The L-5 could also serve as an airborne ambulance.

Four more 44-W-2 WASPs at Gowen were transferred to Smoky Hill Army Air Base in Salina, Kansas, which was a training base for the largest military planes. Mary Ellen Keil and Eleanor Patterson flew on B-17s, one of the heaviest—and most famous—bombers made during World War II. These bombers flew many successful missions in Europe.

Called the *Flying Fortress*, the B-17 carried thirteen machine guns and up to 17,600 lbs. of bombs. The B-17G was 74' 4" in length and had a wingspan of 103' 10". Covered with heavy armor, the bomber weighed 65,500 lbs. and had four 1,200-horse-power engines. The B-17 was most often used to bomb strategic targets in Europe, such as munitions plants and industries. The planes took off from bases in Great Britain and flew deep inside Europe. It took about eight hours to fly to Germany and back.

The first women ever to fly the B-17 were WAFS Nancy Love and Betty Gillies in August 1943. They delivered the bomber from Seattle, Washington to Great Falls, Montana. Seventeen WASPs from 43-W-5 and 43-W-6 were the first to go through B-17 transitional training and actually fly missions. In October 1943, the women pilots arrived at the B-17 training base at Lockbourne Army Air Base in Columbus, Ohio. Of the thirteen women who completed training, nine were assigned as B-17 copilots for gunnery target practice and four remained at Lockbourne as engineering test pilots. The other four went to various bases where they flew multi-engine planes.

In spite of its large size and tremendous weight, the B-17, also called the "Big Friend," was a very safe and stable plane, which was demonstrated to 44-W-2's Eleanor Patterson and Mary Ellen Keil at Salina. They did not go through B-17 training, but they wanted to fly in the big plane. Eleanor struck up a friendship with a major who was a B-17 maintenance test pilot. The night before he was to test a plane, Eleanor talked him into taking her and Mary Ellen with him. They also took another passenger with them: Eleanor's golden retriever that went everywhere she went. For the flight, she had the base parachutist make a parachute for the dog.

On the day of the ride, Mary Ellen sat in the copilot seat while Eleanor and the dog sat in the back. The pilot turned to Mary Ellen and said, "Well, I'm supposed to be up here testing the props, and anyhow, I want to show you how well this plane flies if you lose an engine."

The pilot turned off an engine and the plane handled very well. He cut off the other engine on the same side. Again, the plane was smooth and steady. Then he said, "You know, it will even hold altitude and fly quite well with one engine." And it did, while not loaded with bombs.

The pilot started to shut off the last engine to show how the big plane could glide without power, but he thought better of it. Deciding to test the props, he tried to start the first engine. It would not catch. He tried to bring back the second engine, but no luck. Neither did the third engine start. He turned to the WASPs: "Well, you know, the regulations say that if you have to make a one-engine landing, you have to have the crew jump."

"Jump?" they exclaimed.

They had never jumped from a B-17 and neither had the dog. The major was concerned. "Well," he said, "I'm risking my majority if they catch me landing with one engine and you're still in here, but I'll take a chance that I won't be demoted."[25] Finally, he brought the huge plane in with one engine and made a perfect landing.

Salina Army Air Base in Kansas was also a training base for an even larger bomber, the B-29. The 44-W-2 WASPs did not fly this plane, although Ruth Woods and Mary Ellen transported parts for it. Called the *Superfortress*, this plane weighed 124,000 lbs. and was stuffed with armaments. The wingspan of the B-29 was about 38' wider than the B-17, and it had almost twice the power. This

On the B-29 long-range tests, we carried our heavy dummy load all over the American sky for many hours. Our load had to equal 8,900 pounds and fill an area 10 feet by 28 inches. Now we know these were indeed the measurements needed for the "Little Boy" atom bomb, but we were not supposed to even think it then. Our long-range requirements must have been for a very long flight through the Pacific islands, we thought, perhaps all the way to Tokyo.

Maj. Fred Bretcher was the pilot. I, as one of the alternating copilots, and the rest of the crew were able to watch the light over the land turn pink and then fade into darkness from 30,000 feet. We were then alone with the stars, until dawn crept over the land from the east. The off-watch crew found places to curl up and sleep in the darkened, droning plane. There was a certain boredom as the hours stretched out that would possibly not be present if we were the B-29 chosen to actually deliver the "heavy" bomb.

As part of this project, we made flights from Wright Field to Wendover Field in Utah, where the 509th B-29 Bomb Squadron and Colonels Paul Tibbets and Sweeney awaited parts and repairs for problems on their B-29s resulting from engine overheating. They had been selected to deliver the "heavy" bomb. As the atom-bomb factor was continually denied, we at Wright Field were not subjected to any special secrecy provisions. Our job was to simply make the basic preparatory flight tests and to keep Colonel Tibbets's *Enola Gay* in flying condition with the parts and advice he needed from Wright Field.

Major Bretcher gave me some "left-seat" time in the B-29, with the usual engine-out procedures, though, unfortunately, with not enough time for complete check-off. What I remember most about the B-29 was the fact that the glass nose of the plane distorted the view ahead of the runway. The pilot actually aimed to the side of the runway. Otherwise, except for engine overheating, it was easy to fly.

This casual checking-off in aircraft was usual between Flight Test pilots, and I naturally fell into the process—and felt honored to be included. Flight Test pilots felt a fellow accepted Flight Test pilot was simply qualified to fly airplanes.

Some of the most memorable bomber flights were the evening rides as copilot for Col. James Gillespie in a B-17 (usually the same one). Colonel Gillespie dreaded being forced to accept a generalship and a desk job and not being able to fly anymore. We would go up and fly around, sometimes just sightseeing, sometimes going through various maneuvers. Often, he would turn it over to me to fly while he looked around at the sky and smiled to himself.

Unlike those at FFT, the BFT pilots' wives invited me to join them for family picnics and parties. We went swimming. We went to amusement parks. And sometimes, I went to their Saturday night drinking parties. In fact, if I

judiciously to avoid a stall. In a stall, the plane has lost flying speed and the will to fly.

Bomber Flight Test had several foreign planes to test. The British Lancaster bomber and the plywood Mosquito bomber, as well as the German twin-engine light bomber, the Ju-88. I was able to fly copilot in the Lancaster and Observer copilot in the Mosquito and the Ju-88.

The Mosquito was a small twin-engine bomber. Ours had been built in Canada, and its performance was to be compared with the RAF version from Bascombe Down, England's test base. Pilots seemed to prefer it to the Canadian one.

One morning a Lieutenant F. asked me to fly in a Mosquito with him to record test data. We taxied out and stopped at the end of the runway to go through the pre-takeoff checklist. We went through it several times, and the lieutenant still seemed uncertain, but we took off and ran through some abbreviated tests. I did not feel that the lieutenant was comfortable in the aircraft and was glad to come in and land.

Later, I discussed the flight with one of the FFT pilots, Captain Fountain, I think.

"Oh, Lieutenant F.! Don't fly with him again. Better stick to the old-timers."

I thought perhaps he was joking again, but one afternoon there seemed to be an emergency on the runway. It was a four-engine bomber, with one engine out. It was hard to see what the problem really was, but we saw it approach and then pull up and come around again. That time, however, it crashed beyond the runway, killing all aboard. The pilot had been Lieutenant F.

I was fortunate to be part of two important bomber tests. One was an early air-refueling test. It was an attempt to stretch the range of fighters protecting long-range bomber flights. The other involved heavily loaded, long-range flights in the B-29 Superfortress, to test its capability to carry a new bomb weighing about 9,000 pounds and measuring about 10 feet by 28 inches. Of course we jumped to the conclusion it was for an atom bomb, but we were laughed at. "It's just a heavy bomb," we were told. "No one has an atom bomb yet."

For the air-refueling, I was copilot to Maj. Russ Schleeh, one of BFT's best and most experienced pilots, in the B-24 that acted as tanker. Major Borsodi flew a P-38 Lightning, acting as the plane requiring fuel. While we held the four-engine B-24 in slow flight at about 10,000 feet, Borsodi cut one engine on the P-38 so that he could come close under the B-24 to attach the makeshift nozzle. We had the bomb-bay doors open so that we could look down to see whether he could attach. It was like watching a fish take bait. After several runs, Borsodi started for home. He could not restart his engine, however. We followed him back in case, with only one engine, he was not able to keep the P-38 from cartwheeling into the dead engine. He landed it, however, without incident.

bomber had a range of 3,250 miles. It was with this plane that the Allies finally won the war in the Pacific.

The B-29 was the last bomber developed during the war. Because it was rushed into production, it had "bugs," inherent in almost any new design, that had not been worked out. And this plane had a very big bug: The engines had a tendency to catch fire after takeoff. This was caused by a design flaw in which the cowling, or engine cover, did not have the proper flaps to help cool the engines. Some of the male pilots were skittish about flying this fiery plane.

Paul Tibbets, a young lieutenant colonel at Salina, was in charge of training for the B-29. He looked for two women pilots he could train; he wanted to show the men the plane could be safely flown. He found his two WASPs at Eglin Army Air Base in Florida. Dorothea Johnson and Dora Dougherty were towing targets for gunnery practice at the time; they had no experience piloting four-engine aircraft.

Tibbets told the WASPs about the engine fires, and he showed them how to prevent this problem. The usual preflight procedure was to taxi the plane to the runway and rev the engines for several minutes before takeoff. He instructed the women to taxi the B-29 to the runway and take off immediately, thus eliminating the problem of overheated engines and fires.

When Lt. Colonel Tibbets thought his students were sufficiently trained, he was ready to take the show in the air. He had Fifinella painted on the B-29's nose and named the plane, "Ladybird." He and the WASPs then flew to Clovis Army Air Field in New Mexico where they demonstrated how to fly the B-29. Seeing the women take off and land in the *Superfortress* made an impression. The WASPs put in fifty flying hours until the news reached Washington, D.C., where word came down from on high to get the WASPs out of the B-29 immediately. But they had proved that women were capable of handling the heaviest and most complex of military aircraft.

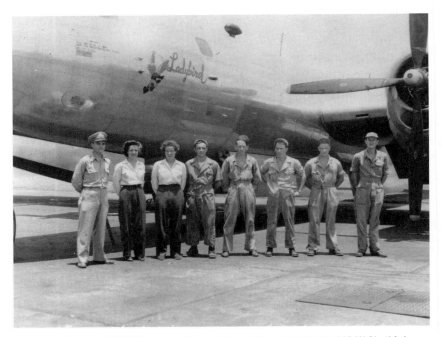

Dorothea Johnson (43-W-4), second from left, and Dora Dougherty (43-W-3), third from left, were the only two WASPs to pilot a B-29 *Superfortress*, which was so enormous that it required five crew members during flights. Their check pilot, Lt. Col. Paul Tibbets, left, would later pilot the *Enola Gay*, the plane that dropped the atomic bomb on Hiroshima, Japan. *Courtesy of The Woman's Collection, Texas Woman's University*

Meanwhile, the 44-W-2 ferry pilots were being reassigned, among them was Susan Clarke. On July 4, 1944, Susan had to deliver a BT-13 from Atlanta, Georgia to Columbia, South Carolina. A second lieutenant at the Atlanta base wanted to catch a ride with her. According to the Army Air Forces accident report, the staff sergeant at the Atlanta Army Air Base told Susan that the plane had not had a preflight check, but she said she did not have time. After fueling the plane, he found the battery was dead and told Susan to run the plane for awhile. With everything seemingly in working order, the passenger climbed in the backseat with his bag and raincoat, and the BT-13 took off.

As the plane approached Columbia, the weather was good with high clouds and a visibility of six miles. At 11:30 A. M., about three miles from the airport, an eyewitness saw the BT-13 and a B-25 flying at the same level, at 1,500 feet. Suddenly, the BT-13 veered to the left and continued going down. The nose hit first and then the left wing. The plane cartwheeled, breaking up and burning as it went.

Susan and her passenger did not survive. Since the plane was totally destroyed, it was difficult for the three investigators to find clues for the cause of the accident. They advanced and discounted several theories: baggage falling and jamming the controls; the passenger being knocked out and throwing his weight on the controls; or pilot and passenger being knocked unconscious. The Army Air Forces investigation finally concluded that the cause of the accident could not be determined.

As a member of 44-W-2, Susan Clarke impressed everyone who knew her. Mrs. Deaton had appointed her as a class officer because of her leadership abilities. Her classmates remembered her as a fine friend and an excellent pilot.

During the latter part of the war, there was greater and greater demand for the pursuit, or fighter planes. More pursuits were produced, and the Army Air Forces needed more pilots to ferry them. About 140 WASPs qualified to fly the pursuits. They ferried more pursuit planes than any other type of aircraft, with the exception of trainer planes.

In World War II, pursuits accompanied bombers during bombing missions, and the pilots engaged in "dogfights" to protect the bomber against enemy planes. They also peeled off to dive through enemy ground fire to strike ships, railroads, and bridges. The pursuits were "hot planes," speedy and unforgiving of mistakes or indecision. It took a pilot with quick reflexes, nerve, and stamina to handle them. Like the men who flew these planes, the women pilots could not be intimidated by them.

Only two 44-W-2 WASPs, Joanne "Jo" Wallace and Ruth Adams, volunteered to fly these fighter planes. They went to Brownsville Pursuit School in Texas for their training. The small cockpit could not accommodate an instructor so the trainee essentially taught herself. The cockpit was intimidating, measuring about 3 x 5 feet, and every inch was filled with knobs, gauges, and dials. With the plane manual in her lap, the trainee studied these instruments and how they were used. And by reading the manual, she taught herself the flight procedure, although sometimes this was done in a classroom.

Jo and Ruth flew seven different types of pursuits, among them was the P-47 *Thunderbolt.* Known as the "Jug" because of its rounded shape, it was the heaviest and fastest of the World War II pursuits. The P-47D weighed a maximum of 19,400 lbs. with armaments. Its 2,800-horsepower engine sent the plane flying at 428 mph. It was used as a bomber escort and to strafe ground targets.

Jo had a horrific experience in a P-47. She had been cleared for takeoff, but as she headed down the runway, another plane taxied in front of her. The impact was so hard that she sheared off the other plane's engine, and her P-47 burst into flames. She tried to escape, but she could not open her hatch. She saw the men on the ground running toward her. Then they stopped because they were afraid the plane would blow up. The cockpit around Jo glowed orange and she felt as if she were being cooked alive. She struggled and fought with the hatch lock.

Finally, she got it open, climbed out on the wing, and fell on the tarmac. Her face was bloodied and her teeth were pushed in when she hit the plane's gunsight. Jo could not feel her nose as the men took her to the infirmary. She was upset about her teeth and worried about her nose, but it was just numb, not missing.

At first officials tried to pin the blame for the accident on Jo, but the control tower had records clearing her for takeoff.

The P-47 *Thunderbolt*, a high altitude fighter and bomber escort, had tremendous fire-power and an ability to survive damage during combat. It had a maximum speed of 428 mph and a range of 590 to 2,000 miles depending on the number of extra fuel tanks. *Courtesy of The Woman's Collection, Texas Woman's University*

Contrary to military regulations which required an investigation for any accident, a formal inquiry was never held. The other pilot continued to fly. Jo did not let this bad experience keep her from flying much-needed pursuits.

Like the other ferry pilots, Marie Michell learned that she would be reassigned from Love Field. While in Dallas, she had fallen in love with Capt. H.C. Robinson, a flight surgeon, and was reluctant to leave. She expressed her apprehensions, hope, and joy in an August 6 letter to her father:

> Anyway, about 50 gals from Dallas are being transferred sometime this week, and none of us know where we're

going. We do know, however, that we will be working for the training command, and that they have too many pilots as it is. I just hope our new jobs aren't a waste of time.

Guess what I'm wearing on my left hand?? My flight surgeon flew down to see me last week—I was out on a trip as usual—but managed to get back a day before he had to leave so we became engaged. . . . I don't know when we'll get married, a lot depends upon my new base, and whether he has to go back to the Southwest Pacific again. But don't worry, I'll keep you posted, you're on my priority 1 list!

Dallas is terribly hot now, perspiration is running all over the place, its almost impossible to sleep at night. How I wish I could spend a few weeks up at Walloon with you, Mmmmmmmmmm that would be wonderful. . . .

Lotsa love,
Marie[26]

Marie Michell would soon learn where her next assignment would be. And the WASPs would also soon know about the status of their program.

THIRTEEN

Flying Higher

I was happiest in the sky—at dawn when the quietness of the air was like a caress, when the noon sun beat down and at dusk when the sky was drenched with the fading light. Think of me there and remember me. . . .

—CORNELIA FORT, WAFS

In August 1944, two months after defeat of the Costello bill in Congress, Jackie Cochran made another attempt to get military status for the WASPs. She sent an eleven-page report on the WASP to Gen. Hap Arnold, which included a brief history of the program, its current status, and some recommendations for its future.

In the report, Jackie again argued that the WASPs should be made a part of the Army Air Forces. If not, she said that "serious consideration should be given to inactivation of the WASP program if militarization is not soon authorized." She went on to say that if the WASPs were inactivated, then the women pilots should "obtain military status, if only for one day, and resulting veterans recognition for all who have served commendably."[27]

Jackie's report was released to the newspapers, which renewed criticism of the WASP program. Some columnists and congressmen again charged that the entire WASP program was a waste of money. Cochran herself was taken to task by some of her own WASPs for delivering what they considered to be an ultimatum to General Arnold. Yet militarizing the WASPs meant getting congressional approval, and he realized that this was probably futile. Also, with the Allied forces achieving successes in Europe, Arnold was now faced with a surplus of returning pilots who could take over ferrying duties.

WASPs were still needed in some crucial jobs. Since few pilots wanted, or even qualified, to fly pursuits, there was a critical shortage of pilots to ferry these planes. The sixty-six WASP pursuit pilots, plus the fifty women pursuit trainees, were desperately needed. In addition, some base commanders depended on women pilots for testing planes, and others needed the WASPs who had advanced instrument training to instruct male cadets. Jackie Cochran decided that it would be unfair to have some WASPs serving with the Army Air Forces, while others could not. It was all or nothing. With great reluctance, General Arnold would make the decision to deactivate the WASP.

While the issue of militarization was being debated, Marie Michell and Kit MacKethan found that they would be reassigned to separate bases. Kit was sent to Cochran Field (not named for Jackie) in Macon, Georgia to test trainer planes. Marie was transferred to Victorville Army Air Field in California to fly training missions for bombardier students. When she arrived on September 18, she was one of eight WASPs at the base.

Victorville Army Air Field was located on the edge of the Mojave Desert. It was an ideal location for bomb training because of the many clear days for flying and because the men could drop live bombs on targets without endangering civilians or damaging property. The base was under the command of Col. Earl Robbins.

Initially, base officials had expressed misgivings about the WASP transfers until they found the eight women had over 500 flying hours each. Even so, the women had to prove themselves before they were accepted. An unnamed base staffer wrote in the report, "History of the WASP Program," "Pilots, Bombardiers and Navigators attached to this station were at first loath to fly with WASP pilots; however . . . all have expressed confidence in the ability and judgment of these young ladies. The distrust and doubt existent at first have been supplanted with the feeling of trust and respect."[28]

The WASPs were initially assigned as test pilots on the BT-13s and as observers to the bombardier section. They were also checked out on the AT-11, a twin-engine plane. This aircraft was used to fly bombardier students on their bombing target practice over the desert. On September 30, the WASPs started a new two-week course, training as bomber pilots. If they passed, they would join 150 male pilots flying practice bombing missions at Victorville.

The accuracy of the bombardiers greatly depended on the pilot's flying accuracy. The pilot had to fly within ten feet of altitude and within half a degree of correct direction. If the pilot did not get over the exact site, the bombardier would miss the target and receive a demerit. Too many demerits, and the bombardier washed out. Bombardier flying was precise, and only three WASPs passed the rigorous course.

After her transfer to Victorville, Marie continued to see newly-promoted Major Robinson, who was stationed in Reno, Nevada. She rode transport planes to meet him at Lake Tahoe on the weekends. Major Robinson also came to visit her at Victorville. They were an attractive couple who kept to themselves. The two had dinner together at the mess hall, took walks, or sat outside on the barrack steps and talked. A rumor floated among some of the WASPs that Marie had married Major Robinson before she came to Victorville.

In a letter to her father, Marie talked about the base and her future plans. The airmail letter was dated October 1, her father's birthday:

Happy Birthday Dad!

Wish I were there to plant a big birthday "burner"! I made a trip into San Bernardino the other day and found a little present for you, hope that it gets there on time and that you like it.

Golly, this base is very nice, even tho its out in the middle of nowhere. I'm in school learning how to fly ships on bombing missions and very shortly will fly bombardiers on practise [*sic*] spins, dropping 100 lb. bombs. Its lots of fun, but we work from 0530 [5:30 A.M.] till 10 at night and really drop into bed at night.

I expect another temporary transfer next month and if it actually comes about will resign at that time—getting tired of being kicked from one base to another. Getting kinda lonesome for my man, too, think I'll get married one of these days! By the way, Hamp's a Major now.

Please tell Grandma that I'm thinking of her and will write soon.

Lots of love,
Marie[29]

At some point, a B-25 *Mitchell* bomber arrived and there was much excitement around the base. Everyone wanted to fly or ride this medium bomber, including Marie. The B-25 was named after Gen. Billy Mitchell who organized the American air force during World War I. The plane was powerful and highly maneuverable. It had two 1,850-horsepower engines and weighed a maximum of 35,000 lbs. The bomber could go 272 mph and had a range of 1,350 miles. Every Allied country used this sturdy, reliable plane during World War II. It was especially important in the Pacific Ocean. Taking off from an aircraft carrier, Gen. James Dolittle led sixteen B-25s on the first bombing raid over Tokyo in April 1942.

October 2, 1944 dawned clear over the Mojave Desert. Marie's roommate had been invited to go up with a friend who had just been checked out on the B-25. But her roommate had a toothache that day, so Marie asked if she could go in her place. She was thrilled to be able to go along for the ride. The pilot was 1st Lt. George Rosado. Marie sat in the copilot's seat and the crew chief sat behind them. After preflighting, they took off about 3:30 in the afternoon.

Twenty-five miles west of the base, a P-39 pilot saw the B-25 flying at 5,000 to 6,000 feet. The plane was spinning, with its nose pointed down. He saw no one bail out from the bomber. The P-39 pilot looked at his watch: It was 3:40 P.M. Another pilot was checking out a student in an AT-6 when they observed the B-25 heading west. They estimated that the bomber was at about 1,000 feet, flying straight and level. The AT-6 pilot looked away, and when he glanced back again he saw the B-25 burning on the ground. He put the plane down as quickly as possible and ran toward the fiery hulk but could not get near because of the intense heat.

The accident report placed the responsibility for the crash on the pilot. The investigator concluded that 1st Lieutenant Rosado had allowed the plane to go into an inadvertent spin and was unable to recover due to insufficient altitude. No one on the B-25 survived the crash. When base officials could remove the three charred bodies from the plane, they found one body with a chain around its neck. On the chain was a wedding ring; Marie had secretly married Major Robinson.

It was a sad day at the base. WASP Margaret Wissler, 43-W-6, had just arrived at the base with students in training. She saw the smoke rising in the distance, and she was told the B-25 had crashed. Margaret had the difficult assignment of packing Marie's things and sending them home. Marie's wardrobe included her wedding trousseau; the clothing was new and exquisite.

Major Robinson accompanied Marie's ashes back home to Michigan for burial. Her family was scattered: Marie's father was in Michigan; her mother lived Washington, D.C. while Marie's stepfather served in the military overseas; Marie's brother, Roy, was stationed at a base in New Jersey. He accompanied his grief-stricken mother to Detroit where memorial services were held. It was then that the family first heard of the marriage to Major Robinson. The couple had planned a large wedding after the war; Marie knew it was what her mother would have wanted.

Kit MacKethan at Cochran Field in Georgia heard about Marie's death. Heartbroken, she tried desperately to get more details by phone, but all she could obtain was that the memorial service for Marie would be held in Detroit. She arranged for a ride on a military transport plane going to Michigan. Then Kit went about her flight duties for the day. In the air, she imagined that Marie was with her. When Kit landed, she entered the operations room, sat down, and wrote a poem in honor of her best friend.

Kit arrived too late for the memorial service. But she fulfilled her pledge to comfort her friend's mother. She read her poem.

CELESTIAL FLIGHT

She is not dead—
But only flying higher,
Higher than she's flown before,
And earthly limitations
Will hinder her no more.

There is no service ceiling,
Or any fuel range,
And there is no anoxia,
Or need for engine change.
Thank God that now her flight can be
To heights her eyes had scanned,
Where she can race with comets,
And buzz the rainbow's span.

For she is universal
Like courage, love and hope,
And all free, sweet emotions
Of vast and godly scope.

And understand a pilot's Fate
Is not the thing she fears,
But rather sadness left behind,
Your heartbreak and your tears.

So all you loved ones, dry your eyes,
Yes, it is wrong that you should grieve,
For she would love your courage more,
And she would want you to believe
She is not dead.
You should have known
That she is only flying higher,
Higher than she's ever flown.

Marie's birthday letter to her father arrived a few days after her memorial service. She was buried in White Chapel Cemetery in Troy, Michigan. Marie Michell Robinson, WASP 44-W-2, was 20 years old at the time of her death. Those who knew her said she was a superb pilot.

Marie Michell completes Form I in the plane's log. Flight Two members remember Marie as a dedicated pilot. *Courtesy of Roy Michell, Jr.*

EPILOGUE

We did what we were supposed to do. . . . We worked hard.
We were necessary—we were useful.

—JEAN MOORE SOARD, WASP 44-W-2

How great that was!

—ESTHER E. NOFFKE, WASP 44-W-2

A few days after Marie Michell Robinson's death on October 2, 1944, all of the WASPs received two letters: one was from Director Jacqueline Cochran stating that the WASP program was being deactivated, effective December 20, 1944; the other letter was from Gen. Hap Arnold, expressing his appreciation for the WASPs' service to their country.

The last class at Avenger, 44-W-10, graduated December 7, 1944, three years to the day after Pearl Harbor was bombed. Avenger Field sported new barracks and new hangers. Electric lights lined the new runways, replacing the flares. General Arnold gave the final commencement address:

I want to stress how valuable I believe the whole WASP program has been for the country. . . . But please understand
that I do not look upon the WASP and the job they have
done in this war as a project or an experiment. A pioneer-
ing venture, yes, solely an experiment, no. The WASP are an
accomplishment. . . . We of the Army Air Forces are proud
of you; we will never forget our debt to you.[30]

The next day, the commander of Avenger Field ordered the
sixty-eight graduates into their flight gear and told them to fly
the remaining trainer planes to the military base at San Angelo,
Texas. It was their first and last ferrying duty. Then they went
home. No severance pay, no military benefits. It would be more
than thirty years before women would again pilot military
planes.

At Long Beach, California, forty-five women flew to the very
end. When they left, squadron commander Barbara Erickson
closed her office door and walked past sixty-one shiny new P-51s
that needed to be delivered. Las Vegas Army Air Field threw a big
party for its WASPs. In La Junta, Colorado, 44-W-2's Anne Berry
went to her commander's office to pay her last respects. He said,
"Well, you didn't mess up too much."[31]

World War II ended in August 1945. With its cities in ruins,
Germany surrendered May 7. The Japanese continued fighting
until the United States dropped atomic bombs on the cities of
Hiroshima and Nagasaki. They finally surrendered on August 14.
America and its allies had won the war, and air power had played
a major role, just as General Arnold predicted.

After the war ended, AT-6s and C-47s continued service. AT-
6s were sold to many countries around the world and remained
in use for at least forty years after they were first introduced. A
few World War II aircraft were sold to individuals or groups who
restored them. But most planes were scrapped, melted down, and

turned into toasters, refrigerators, automobiles, and other consumer goods that a postwar generation wanted.

The day after the WASP program was deactivated, Hap Arnold was promoted from general of the Army Air Forces to general of the Army, earning his fifth star. In 1947, the Air Force was made a separate military service, and General Arnold was its first head. When he died of heart failure in 1950, he was lauded as the father of the modern Air Force.

After the WASP disbandment, Jackie Cochran became a war correspondent in the Pacific for *Liberty* magazine. She witnessed the Japanese surrender in the Philippines and was the first woman correspondent to enter Japan after World War II. She also attended the Nuremberg war crimes trial, when the Nazi leadership had to answer for their atrocities.

Then she went back to chasing more air records. In 1953, she became the first woman to break the sound barrier. In 1962, she was the first woman to fly a jet plane across the Atlantic Ocean. When she was in her late fifties, she set nine international speed, distance, and altitude records in a T-38 jet. And she broke some of her own records flying the F-104 Lockheed *Starfighter*—one of the most dangerous planes ever made because of its design.

During her lifetime, Jackie Cochran was awarded many aviation honors. France bestowed its Legion of Honor and the French Air Medal on her. In this country, she was given a Distinguished Service Medal for her work during the war. The Air Force conferred on her the rank of lieutenant colonel. She was awarded the Legion of Merit and three Distinguished Flying Crosses, among other honors. In 1971, she was inducted into the Aviation Hall of Fame. When she died in 1980, Jackie Cochran held more speed, altitude, and distance records than any pilot—male or female—in aviation history.

In December 1944, Nancy Love became the first woman to check out the four-engine transport plane, the C-54 *Skymaster,* after only three hours of instruction. She delivered three of the big planes before the WASP was deactivated. During her more than two years of service, she checked out almost every kind of aircraft made during World War II. The Air Force made her a colonel, and she later received the Air Medal. After the war, she embarked on a flight around the world and flew half the distance by herself. She and her husband moved to Martha's Vineyard in Massachusetts and had three daughters. In 1976 she died of cancer at the age of 62.

Leoti Deedie Deaton resumed her career with the Red Cross. She taught swimming and water safety to thousands of people over a period of sixty years with this organization. For her years of service, she was awarded the Red Cross Golden Whale Award, and she was inducted into the International Lifesaving Hall of Fame. Until her death in 1986, she remained active in the WASP organization.

Dr. Nels O. Monserud, who studied the WASPs, was promoted to captain and made chief flight surgeon at Avenger Field. After deactivation, he compiled studies of the relationship of female physiology on flying abilities. His report to the U.S. Army Air Forces surgeon general was an important scientific study in medical aviation.

The report concluded that a woman's menses did not interfere with her flying abilities. He found that women pilots' physical stamina and endurance were excellent. The WASPs had fewer lost flying days due to fatigue than the male pilots. Emotional disturbances due to stress of flying were rare.

His findings were confirmed by reports from various bases. The commander of the Fifth Ferrying Group in Dallas said that the WASPs were dependable and not easily distracted. The flight surgeon noted, "At Love Field, for all causes WASPs lost less than .1 day per girl per month."[32] At Victorville, Marie Michell Robinson's base, the WASPs flew fifty to seventy hours a month. The base commander said flying personnel expressed confidence in the WASPs' ability and judgment. The adjutant there noted that they were eager, enthusiastic, cooperative, and emotionally well-balanced.

What did the WASPs accomplish during their twenty-seven months of existence during World War II? Out of 1,830 women chosen for the WASP program (25,000 had applied), 1,074 graduated in eighteen different classes. The women pilots served at over 120 air fields in the United States. They flew more than sixty million miles in every type of aircraft made at the time. By doing so, they freed the male pilots for crucial combat duty. Thirty-eight WASPs lost their lives, either during training or service.

In 1972, the WASPs held their first national reunion in Sweetwater, Texas. At their next reunion two years later, they discussed mounting a new campaign for military recognition. In 1976 when women cadets were admitted to the Air Force Academy, the media greeted the news with great fanfare, saying that women would fly military planes for the first time. Not so, said the WASPs—we were the first! Then the women flew into obtaining military status for themselves—over thirty years after their organization was disbanded.

It was no easier getting congressional approval the second time around. Representative Lindy Boggs of Louisiana and Senator Barry Goldwater of Arizona, who was a ferry pilot at New Castle Army Air Base in Delaware, guided the militarization measure through Congress. It was sponsored by every woman serving in Congress and was supported by the Defense Department and the Air Force. Also giving his support was Col. Bruce Arnold, son of Gen. Hap Arnold. The bill was opposed by the American Legion, the Veterans Administration, and some members of Congress, many of whom were former veterans. They argued that if they conferred veteran status to these civilian women pilots, then other civilian organizations who served during World War II would demand to be given veterans benefits.

After several failed attempts to move the bill out of committee, Senator Goldwater attached it as an amendment to a veterans bill. It passed, and on November 23, 1977, President Jimmy Carter signed the bill into law. Yet many of the military benefits were not retroactive.

In 1979, with the approval of Congress, the secretary of the Air Force announced that WASPs would be considered veterans. They were now eligible for veterans' benefits, although their home buying and education needs were long behind them. But they were finally being recognized for their war contributions.

After the war, only about a quarter of the WASPs remained in aviation. Flying was too expensive for many, and most of the piloting jobs went to men. The commercial airlines refused to hire women as pilots and instead offered them jobs as stewardesses. Some became flight and instrument instructors at local airports and flight schools, while others worked for aircraft companies. A few WASPs had trouble adjusting to the disbandment. On the first anniversary of deactivation, one committed suicide.

Some WASPs entered the military services or enrolled in the military reserves of the navy, army, air force, and marines. The first woman to pilot a military jet plane was Ann Baumgartner Carl, WASP 43-W-5. Some became businesswomen, while others went into teaching, law, and medicine. They also became artists, writers, musicians, and sculptors. Others chose careers in sports. Many of the women married and threw their considerable energies and talents into their families and communities.

One-third of Marie Michell's class of 44-W-2 remained active in aviation: six were flight and instruments instructors at private airports; one taught with the Civil Air Patrol; two managed their own flight schools; and two were copilots on business planes. Three went back to flight school and earned their commercial pilot's licenses. Gini Dulaney Campbell set distance and altitude glider records at 30,000 feet. Some flew their own planes into their seventies!

A few members of 44-W-2 went into social work, while others became teachers. Nearly all did volunteer work in their communities. At least two worked in publishing as editors and writers. One was a psychiatrist, and several owned their own businesses. Most of the WASPs had more than one career during their lifetime. But not one ever lost her interest in aviation.

The 44-W-2 women were also mothers, and many named their daughters after their former classmates. One baymate of Marie Michell Robinson named her daughter after Marie. To honor Marie's memory, Roy Michell, Sr. established a scholarship fund at the University of Michigan. The daughter of one 44-W-2 WASP attended college with the benefit of this scholarship.

In spite of prejudice and discrimination, the WASPs persevered and made a contribution during World War II. While a younger generation of women military pilots hailed them as heroes and role models, the WASPs saw themselves as pilots who served their nation. They believed that they were necessary and useful—and so they were. The WASPs' zest for adventure, their strong sense of self, and their love of flying and country still remain. Their spirit and legacy fly ever higher.

APPENDIX 1

44-W-2 Graduates

Listed alphabetically by maiden name, which is underlined.

Ruth <u>Adams</u>
Anne (Beets) E. <u>Berry</u> Lesnikowski
Susan P. <u>Clarke</u>
Maisie Kay <u>Cleverly</u> Browning
Annabelle <u>Craft</u> Moss
Virginia (Gini) E. <u>Dulaney</u> Campbell
Twila E. <u>Edwards</u> Andrews
Margaret <u>Ehlers</u> Twito
Doris <u>Elkington</u> Hamaker
L. Marjorie (Marge) <u>Gilbert</u> Stewart
Leona (Lee) <u>Golbinec</u> Zimmer
Mildred (Millie) W. <u>Grossman</u> Palmer
Kate Lee <u>Harris</u> Adams
Jean <u>Hascall</u> Cole
Dorothy (Sadie) <u>Hawkins</u> Goot
Mary (Minkie) L. <u>Heckman</u>
Annelle (Nellie) <u>Henderson</u> Bulechek
Kathryn F. <u>Herman</u>

Marjorie (Marge) <u>Johnson</u>

Mary Ellen <u>Keil</u>

Frances (Fran) <u>Laraway</u> Smith

Beverly (Betty) M. <u>LeFevre</u>

Muriel (Mimi) <u>Lindstrom</u> Segall

Verda-Mae (Skippy) <u>Lowe</u> Jennings

Elizabeth (Kit) <u>MacKethan</u> Magid

Mary J. <u>McCrae</u> McCallum

Marie <u>Michell</u> Robinson

Alice M. <u>Montgomery</u>

Harriet Jean <u>Moore</u> Soard

Margaret (Marge) <u>Needham</u> Walker

Esther E. <u>Noffke</u>

Eleanor J. <u>Patterson</u> Brady

Ruth Mary <u>Petry</u>

Anna Mae <u>Petteys</u> Pattee

Rose Lourette <u>Puett</u> Potter

Rose D. <u>Reese</u>

Jane <u>Rutherford</u> Wiswell

Mary (Sandy) <u>Saunders</u> Willson

Clarice (Sid) I. <u>Siddall</u> Bergemann

M. Frances (Smitty) <u>Smith</u> Tuchband

Yvonne (Shorty) M. <u>Stafford</u>

Betty Pauline <u>Stine</u>

Mary V. <u>Strok</u> Peter

Madeline <u>Sullivan</u> O'Donnell

Phyllis (Toby) <u>Tobias</u> Felker

Joanne (Jo) <u>Wallace</u> Orr

Ruth <u>Weller</u> Kunkle

M. Joan <u>Whelan</u> Lyle

Ruth M. <u>Woods</u>

Lorraine (Zilch) H. <u>Zillner</u> Rodgers

WASP Fatalities

Jane D. Champlin, 43-4*
Susan P. Clarke, 44-2
Marjorie L. Davis, 44-9*
Katherine A. Dussaq, 44-1
Marjorie D. Edwards, 44-6*
Jayne E. Erickson, 44-6*
Cornelia Fort, WAFS
Frances F. Grimes, 43-3
Mary P. Hartson, 43-5
Mary H. Howson, 44-4*
Edith C. Keene, 44-1
Kathryn B. Lawrence, 43-8*
Hazel Ying Lee, 43-4
Paula R. Loop, 43-2
Alice E. Lovejoy, 43-5
Peggy W. Martin, 44-4
Lea Ola McDonald, 43-4*
Virginia Moffatt, 43-2
Beverly Moses, 44-5

Dorothy M. Nichols, 43-2
Jeanne L. Norbeck, 44-3
Margaret Oldenburg, 43-4
Mabel Rawlinson, 43-3
Gleanna Roberts, 44-9
Marie Michell Robinson, 44-2
Bettie M. Scott, 44-3
Dorothy F. Scott, WAFS
Margaret J. Seiip, 43-5*
Helen J. Severson, 43-5*
Marie E. Sharon, 43-4
Evelyn Sharp, WAFS
Betty P. Stine, 44-2*
Marion Toevs, 43-8
Gertrude Tompkins, 43-7
Mary Trebing, 43-4
Mary L. Webster, 44-8
Bonnie J. Welz, 43-6
Betty T. Wood, 43-4

---

* Trainee

APPENDIX 3

Selected World War II Aircraft Flown by WASPs

Type of Plane

Number	*Name*	*Use*
LIAISON		
L-1	*Vigilant*	glider, spotter
L-2	*Grasshopper*	glider tow, spotter
L-3	*Grasshopper*	glider tow, liaison
L-4	*Grasshopper*	glider tow, spotter
L-5	*Sentinel*	liaison, ambulance
L-6	*Cadet*	liaison, utility
TRAINERS		
PT-13	*Kaydet*	primary trainer
PT-26	*Cornell*	primary trainer
PT-21	*Recruit*	primary trainer
BT-9	*Yale*	basic trainer
BT-13	*Valiant*	basic trainer
AT-6	*Texan*	advanced trainer

Type of Plane

Number	*Name*	*Use*
TRAINERS		
AT-10	*Wichita*	advanced trainer
AT-11	*Kansan*	bombardier trainer, cargo
AT-17	*Bobcat*	advanced trainer, cargo
AT-18	*Hudson*	trainer, light bomber
AT-19	*Reliant*	advanced trainer, transport
TRANSPORT		
C-46	*Commando*	cargo
C-47	*Skytrain*	cargo
C-54	*Skymaster*	cargo
C-60	*Lodestar*	cargo, light bomber
C-76	*Caravan*	cargo
BOMBERS		
B-17	*Flying Fortress*	heavy bomber
B-18	*Bold*	patrol bomber
B-24	*Liberator*	heavy bomber
B-25	*Mitchell*	medium bomber
B-26	*Marauder*	medium bomber
B-29	*Superfortress*	heavy bomber
A-20	*Havoc*	attack bomber
A-24	*Dauntless*	attack bomber
A-25	*Helldiver*	attack bomber

Type of Plane

Number	*Name*	*Use*
PURSUITS		
P-38	*Lightning*	fighter
P-39	*Airacobra*	fighter
P-40	*Warhawk*	fighter
P-47	*Thunderbolt*	fighter, bomber escort
P-51	*Mustang*	fighter, bomber escort
P-61	*Black Widow*	night fighter
P-63	*Kingcobra*	fighter
EXPERIMENTAL		
YPQ-12		drone
PQ-8 and PQ-14		drone targets
YP-59A		jet

NOTES

1. Jean Hascall Cole, *Women Pilots of World War II* (Salt Lake City: University of Utah Press, 1992), 24.
2. Ibid., 14.
3. Ibid.
4. Doris Brinker Tanner, *Zoot Suits and Parachutes* (Paducah, Ky.: Turner Publishing Co., 1996), 16.
5. Leni Leoti Clark Deaton, interview by Ziggy Hunter, March 18, 1975, edited by Dawn Letson (Denton: Texas Woman's University, The Woman's Collection, Mss. 300), 61.
6. Jacqueline Cochran, *The Stars at Noon* (London: Robert Hale, Ltd., 1955), 46.
7. Jacqueline Cochran and Maryann B. Brinley, *Jackie Cochran: The Autobiography of the Greatest Woman Pilot in Aviation History* (New York: Bantam Books, 1987), 113.
8. Ibid., 132.
9. Ibid., book jacket.
10. Ibid., 200.
11. Lorraine Zillner Rodgers, interview by Jean Hascall Cole, June 19, 1989 (Denton: Texas Woman's University, The Woman's Collection, Mss. 300c), 3.

12. Cole, 57.
13. Ibid., 64.
14. Deaton, 23.
15. Ibid., 24.
16. Thomas Coffey, *Hap: The Story of the United States Air Force and the Man Who Built It* (New York: The Viking Press 1977), 47.
17. Tanner, 110-111.
18. Cole, 73.
19. Ibid., 4.
20. WASP, *WASP "Songbook"* (n.d.), 38.
21. Cole, 111.
22. Ibid., 110.
23. Ibid.
24. Rodgers, 5.
25. Cole, 96.
26. Marie Michell Robinson, letter to her father, August 6, 1944.
27. Quote in Byrd Howell Granger, *On Final Approach: The Women Airforce Service Pilots of WWII* (Scottsdale, Ariz.: Falconer Publishing Co., 1991), 391.
28. "History of WASP Program" (Victorville, Cal.: Victorville Army Air Field, 23 August to 20 December 1944), 4.
29. Marie Michell, letter to her father, October 1, 1944.
30. Tanner, 158-159.
31. Cole, 131.
32. U.S. Army Air Forces, Office of the Air Surgeon, *Report of Air Surgeon's Office on WASP Personnel* (no place given, 1945), 26.

GLOSSARY

AAC—Army Air Corps, aviation division of the Army until 1942.

ATA—Air Transport Auxiliary; Great Britain's World War II civilian pilots' organization.

ATC—Air Transport Command; WASPs served in this Army Air Forces command structure.

B-4 BAG—pilot's canvas bag that could be hung in the plane.

BARNSTORMER—pilot who toured the country performing aerial stunts and giving passenger rides.

CATTLE WAGON—military van that transported pilot trainees, principally from base to auxiliary field.

CIVIL SERVICE—federal division of civilian employees.

CO—Commanding Officer of military base.

DRAG—any force on or against a moving aircraft that slows it down; ice on a plane causes drag.

FLAPS—moveable hinged surfaces on the edge of a plane's wings; flaps are lowered to make the plane fly more slowly.

FORM I—airplane log.

FUSELAGE—body of the plane.

G.I.—Government Issue; items given to military personnel; also came to stand for the person who received them during World War II.

GOSPORT—tube connecting earphones and voice cone; communication device used in planes with no radio.

HOOD—black hood that fit over the cockpit; used to teach instrument flying.

INSTRUMENT FLYING—using a plane's instruments to fly. Used when visual flying is not possible.

LINK TRAINER—training device that allowed a student pilot to practice instrument flying without leaving the ground.

LOGBOOK—record of a pilot's flight time.

RUDDER—hinged, moveable portion of the tail that makes the plane change directions.

SPIN—maneuver where aircraft descends, spinning around its vertical axis.

STALL—a condition that occurs when the plane loses airspeed, causing the wings to lose lift; the nose then drops and the plane loses altitude.

STICK—controls of a plane, used to make aircraft go up or down.

TOW TARGET—towed behind a plane to help train gunners; either a large, flat, steel rectangle or a cloth sleeve.

TOWER—air field's central unit that directs and controls air traffic.

TRANSITION TRAINING—a short period of time during which the pilot is taught to fly certain military aircraft.

WAC—Women's Army Corps; women's Army division during World War II.

WAFS—Women's Auxiliary Ferry Squadron; women civilian pilots organized in Sept. 1942, under the command of Nancy Love.

WASH OUT—failure to complete training.

WASP—Women Airforce Service Pilots; organization created by combining WAFS and WFTD in Nov. 1943, under the direction of Jackie Cochran.

WFTD—Women's Flying Training Detachment; Jackie Cochran's original women pilot training program; organized Sept. 1942.

SELECTED BIBLIOGRAPHY

Listed are the major sources out of approximately 100 that were used in the research of this book.

Ambrose, Stephen E. *D-Day, June 6, 1944: The Climactic Battle of World War II.* New York: Simon & Schuster, 1994.

Boyne, Walker. *The Smithsonian Book of Flight.* Washington, D.C.: Smithsonian Institution Press, 1987.

Carl, Ann B. *A Wasp Among Eagles.* Washington, D.C.: Smithsonian Institution Press, 1999.

Cochran, Jacqueline. "Final Report on Women Pilot Training Program." Washington, D.C.: Headquarters Army Air Force, undated.

————. *The Stars at Noon.* London: Robert Hale, Ltd., 1955.

———— and Maryann B. Brinley. *Jackie Cochran: The Autobiography of the Greatest Woman Pilot in Aviation History.* New York: Bantam Books, 1987.

Coffey, Thomas. *Hap: The Story of the United States Air Force and the Man Who Built It.* New York: Viking Press, 1977.

Cole, Jean Hascall. Jean Hascall Cole Collection. Denton: Texas Woman's University, The Woman's Collection, Mss 138c, 1989-1990.

————. *Women Pilots of World War II*. Salt Lake City: University of Utah Press, 1992.

Deaton, Leni Leoti Clark. Interview by Ziggy Hunter. In WASP Oral History Project edited by Dawn Letson. Denton: Texas Woman's University, The Woman's Collection, Mss. 300, March 18, 1975.

Douglas, Deborah. *United States Women in Aviation, 1940-1985*. Washington D.C.: Smithsonian Institution Press, 1991.

Granger, Byrd Howell. *On Final Approach: The Women Airforce Service Pilots of WWII*. Scottsdale, Ariz.: Falconer Publishing Co., 1991.

Haynsworth, Leslie and David Toomey. *Amelia Earhart's Daughters: The Wild and Glorious Story of American Women Aviators from World War II to the Dawn of the Space Age*. New York: William Morrow and Co., 1998.

"History of WASP Program." Victorville, Cal.: Victorville Army Air Field, 23 August 1944 to 20 December 1944.

Hodgson, Marion S. *Winning My Wings*. Annapolis, Md.: Naval Institute Press, 1996.

Keil, Sally Van Wagenen. *Those Wonderful Women in Their Flying Machines*. New York: Four Directions Press, 1990.

Magid, Ken. *Women of Courage*. Videocassette. Lakewood, Colo.: KM Productions, 1993.

McGuire, Nina and Sandra Sammons. *Jacqueline Cochran: America's Fearless Aviator*. Lake Buena Vista, Fla.: Tailored Tours, 1997.

Noggle, Anne. *A Dance With Death*. College Station: Texas A & M University Press, 1994.

Pateman, Lt. Col. (Ret.) Yvonne. *Women Who Dared: American Female Test Pilots, Flight-Test Engineers, and Astronauts, 1912-1996*. Portland, Oreg.: Norstahr Publishing, 1997.

Robinson, Marie Michell. Two letters dated August 6, 1944 and October 1, 1944.

Rodgers, Lorraine Zillner. Transcript of interview by Jean
Hascall Cole. Denton: Texas Woman's University, The
Woman's Collection, Mss. 300, June 19, 1989.

Tanner, Doris B., comp. *Who Were the WASP?: A World War II
Record.* Sweetwater, Tex.: *The Sweetwater Reporter,* 1989.

———. *Zoot Suits and Parachutes.* Paducah, Ky.: Turner
Publishing Co., 1996.

Taylor, Michael, comp. and ed. *Jane's Encyclopedia of Aviation.*
New York: Portland House, 1989.

U. S. Army Air Forces. Office of the Air Surgeon. *Report to Air
Surgeon's Office on WASP Personnel.* Maxwell Air Force Base,
Ala.: Air Force Historical Research Agency, 1945.

Verges, Marianne. *On Silver Wings: The Women Airforce Service
Pilots of World War II, 1942-1944.* New York: Ballantine Books,
1991.

War Department. U.S. Army Air Forces. Accident Reports.
Maxwell Air Force Base, Ala.: Air Force Historical Research
Agency.

———. #44-2-25-38, Betty Pauline Stine, 25 Feb. 1944.

———. #45-7-4-15, Susan Clarke, 4 July 1944.

———. #45-10-2-3, Marie Michell Robinson, 2 Oct. 1944.

WASP. *WASP "Songbook."* n.d.

WGBH Educational Foundation: The American Experience. *The
Fly Girls.* Videocassette. Boston, Mass.: A Silver Lining
Production Film, 1999.

Williams, Vera. *WASPs: Women Airforce Service Pilots in World War
II.* Osceola, Wis.: Motorbooks International, 1994.

Wood, Winifred. *We Were WASPs.* Coral Gables, Fla.: Glade
House, 1945.

INDEX

Pages with photographs appear in boldface type. WASPs discussed in text are cited here; a complete list of 44–W–2 WASP graduates can be found in Appendix 1.

Adams, Ruth, 96
Airplanes (by number): A-24 *Dauntless,* **68**; AT-6 *Texan,* 40, 44, **48**, 108; B-17 *Flying Fortress,* 64, **82**, 86, 91–92; B-24 *Liberator,* 67–69, **76**, 86; B-25 *Mitchell,* 102–03; B-26 *Marauder,* 64, 65–70; B-29 *Superfortress,* 92–93, **94**; BT-13 (BT-15) *Vultee,* 15, 38–39, 44, 94–95; C-47 *Skytrain,* 86–87, 108; P-47 *Thunderbolt,* 96, **97**; PT-13 *Kaydet,* **30**; PT-19A *Fairchild,* 29, 30, 31, **58**, 87. *See also* Primary trainers; Pursuits

Archer, Virginia Williams, **82**
Army Air Forces Strategic Command School, 89–90
Arnold, Henry H. (Hap), 24–25, 26, 27, 54, 55–56, 59–62, **61**; involvement in WASP militarization, 76–77, 99–100; speeches, 59–60, 107–08; postwar, 109
Avenger Field (Texas), 1, 3, 4, **5**–7, 8, 9, 10–11, 28; civilian staff, 12, 31, 44–45; closed, 107–08; conditions at, 32, 43–44; graduations, 28, 42, 54–55, 56–62, **61**; inspections at, 35–36; military staff, 11, 33; trainees at, **2**, **12**, **30**, **34**, **37**, **106**

Berry, Anne, **12**, 86, 108
Bill H.R. 4219, 47, 75, 76–77
British Air Transport Auxiliary (ATA), 26

129

Campbell, Gini. *See* Dulaney, Gini

Church, Pat, 32–33

Clarke, Susan, **12**, 94–95

Cochran, Jacqueline (Jackie), 15–23, **20**; childhood and youth, 15–16; as aviator, 3, 17–19, 21–23, 109; as businesswoman, 19–21; marriage, 21; involvement with ATA, 25–26; as WFTD director, 25–26, 27; at Avenger Field, 14, 28, 54, 56, 59, 61–62; as WASP director, 3–4, **20**, 27–28, 54, 64, 89–90; efforts for WASP militarization, 28, 46–47, 99–100; postwar, 109; death, 109

Cole, Jean. *See* Hascall, Jean

Davidson, Mildred, **76**

Deaton, Leni Leoti Clark (Deedie): as chief establishment officer, 7–9, 10, 14, 28, 34, 36, 42, 43, 50, 63–64, 78; at graduations, 54, 56, 60; postwar, 110

Dougherty, Dora, 93, **94**

Dulaney (Campbell), Gini, **12**, 73–75, 112–13

Earhart, Amelia, 3, 18–19

Ehlers, Margaret, **12**, 86

Elkington (Hamaker), Doris, 73–75

Erickson, Barbara, 60, 108

Fifinella, **5**, 93, **94**

44-W-2, 1–7, **2**, **12**–14; cross-country flights, 46–52; curriculum of, 12–13, 35; discrimination against, 76–78, 96–97; as engineering test pilots, 71–75; as ferry pilots, 79–88; graduation of, 54–55, 56–62, **61**; inspections of, 35–36; and instrument training, 38, 40–42, **41**, 44; and intermediate training, 38–45; and Link training, 38, 40–42, **41**; and night flying, 44–45; postwar, 112–13; prejudice against, 31, 33, 44–45, 67, 72, 74, 76–78; and primary training, 29–37; service assignments, 64–75, 78–80, 86–89, 90–92, 94–98; uniforms of, 13–14, 53–54, **61**, **76**; and washouts, 6, 33–34

Gilbert, Marge, **12**, 69–70

Golbinec, Leona, **12**, 60–61, 72

Hamaker, Doris. *See* Elkington, Doris

Harris, Kate Lee, **12**, 60–61, 72

Hascall (Cole), Jean, 7, **12**, 44–45, 79

Hawkins, Dorothy "Sadie," 6, **12**, 69

Henderson, Nellie, 7, **12**

Huffhines, Eloise, **76**

Johnson, Dorothea, 93, **94**

Keil, Mary Ellen, **12**, 70, 91–92

LaRue, William, 11, 31, 34

Lindstrom, Muriel, **12**, 86

Love Field (Texas), 64, 79–81, 85

Love, Nancy, 10, 27, 57–59, **58**, 109–10

Lowe, Verda-Mae, 49

MacKethan, Elizabeth "Kit," 1, 3, 7, 37, 39, 42; service, **76**, 79, 80–86, 90, 100, 104; poem by, 104–05

Marsh, Clara Jo, **76**

McCrae, Mary, 86

Michell (Robinson), Marie, 1–3, **2**, 4–5, 6, **106**, 113; WASP training, 29, 37, 42, 44; WASP graduation, 53, 56, 60; WASP service, 64, 79, 80, 90, 97–98, 100, 101–03; letters of, 97–98, 102; marriage, 101–03; death, 103–05

Militarization, 47, 75, 76–77, 99–100, 111–12. *See also* Bill H.R. 4219

Military Affairs Committee, 75, 76–77

Military check rides, 33, 34

Moffatt, Virginia, 36–37

Monserud, Nels, 11, 110

Montgomery, Alice, 86

Morse code, 35, 40–41, 42

Noffke, Esther, 66

Patterson, Eleanor "Pat," 69–70, 91–92

Petry, Ruth, 73

Primary trainers, 30, 58, 81, 83

Pursuits, 95–96, 97, 100, 108

Robinson, Marie. *See* Michell, Marie

Smith, Fran, 51, 66, 68–69

Soviet women combat pilots, 26, 90

Stafford, Yvonne "Shorty," 49–50, 79

Stine, Betty Pauline, 51–52

Strok, Mary, 51, 73

Sullivan, Madeline, 66, 69

Sweetwater, Texas, 1, 3, 9, 10, 36

Tibbets, Paul, 93, **94**

Tobias, Phyllis, 87

U. S. Army Air Forces, 3, 27; accident reports of, 52, 95, 103; created, 56; and discrimination against WASPs, 96–97; and prejudice against WASPs, 10–11, 33, 67; and staff at Avenger Field, 6, 10–11; and WASP militarization, 75, 76–77

Victorville Army Air Field (California), 100–03, 110–11

WAFS. *See* Women's Auxiliary Ferry Squadron

Wallace, Joanne "Jo," 96–97

WASP. *See* Women Airforce Service Pilots

WFTD. *See* Women's Flying Training Detachment

Whelan, Joan, 68–69

Wishing Well, 32, **34**

Women Airforce Service Pilots (WASP), 1–4, **2**, 5, 6; accomplishments of, 111, 112–13; and civilian status, 11, 27–28, 64; creation of, 27–28; deactivation of, 100, 107–08; deaths of, 36–37, 51–52, 94–95, 103–05; discrimination against, 28, 67, 72, 74, 76–78, 96–97, 100, 111, 113; evaluations of, 110–11; and flying regulations, 83; graduations of, 14–15, 54–55, 56–62, **61**, 107–08; inspections of, 35–36; and militarization efforts, 28, 46–47, 54–55, 75–77, 99–100, 111–12; and officer training, 89–90; pilot's equipment, 65, 80–81; postwar, 112–13; prejudice against, 10–11, 31, 33, 44–45; requirements, 4; rules, 14; service, 64–70, **68**, 71–75, 79–88, **82**, 90–93, **94**, 96–**97**, 100–101; songs of, 34, 62; training, 6, 11–14, 27–36, **37**, 38–42, **41**, 44–45, 46–52; uniforms, 13–14, 53–54, **61**, **76**, 84; wages, 4, 80

Women's Auxiliary Ferry Squadron (WAFS), 10, 27, 57–59, **58**

Women's Flying Training Detachment (WFTD), 9–10, 25–26, 27

Woods, Ruth, 70

World War II, 3, 24, 26–27, 56, 63, 108; battles, 38, 53, 87; women's roles during, 26–27

Zillner, Lorraine, 39–40, 43, **61**, 79